Getting Started with SQL
A Hands-on Approach for Beginners

Thomas Nield

Beijing · Boston · Farnham · Sebastopol · Tokyo

Getting Started with SQL

by Thomas Nield

Copyright © 2016 Thomas Nield. All rights reserved.

Printed in the United States of America.

Published by O'Reilly Media, Inc., 1005 Gravenstein Highway North, Sebastopol, CA 95472.

O'Reilly books may be purchased for educational, business, or sales promotional use. Online editions are also available for most titles (*http://safaribooksonline.com*). For more information, contact our corporate/institutional sales department: 800-998-9938 or *corporate@oreilly.com*.

Editor: Shannon Cutt
Production Editor: Shiny Kalapurakkel
Copyeditor: Jasmine Kwityn
Proofreader: Rachel Head

Indexer: Ellen Troutman-Zaig
Interior Designer: David Futato
Cover Designer: Randy Comer
Illustrator: Rebecca Demarest

February 2016:   First Edition

Revision History for the First Edition
2016-02-08:   First Release

See *http://oreilly.com/catalog/errata.csp?isbn=9781491938614* for release details.

978-1-491-93861-4

[LSI]

Table of Contents

Foreword

Over the past three decades, computers have taken over the world. Twenty-five years ago, we lived analog. We communicated using an analog POTS telephone, we tuned in to analog FM radio stations, and we went to the library and browsed the stacks for information. Buildings were constructed using hand-drawn blueprints; graphic artists worked with pen, brush, and ink; musicians plucked strings and blew into horns and recorded on analog tape; and airplanes were controlled by physical cables connecting the yoke to the control surfaces.

But now everything is computerized and digital. Consequently, every member of society needs to be familiar with computers. That does not mean having the deep knowledge of a techie, but just as poets need to study a little math and physics, and just as mathematicians need to read a little poetry, so too does everybody today need to know something about computers.

I think that this book really helps to address the knowledge gap between techies and laypeople, by providing an accessible and easy-to-read discussion of SQL—a core database technology.

—Richard Hipp, Creator of SQLite

Preface

Nobody needs to learn how a car engine works in order to drive a car. The whole point of technologies like SQL is to allow you to focus on the business problem, and not worry about how the technical details are executed. This book will give you a practical focus on using SQL, and will steer away from unnecessary technical details that are likely not pertinent to your immediate needs. Much of the content revolves around hands-on exercises with real databases you can download so you see how concepts are applied. When you finish this book you will have practical knowledge to work with databases, as well as use them to overcome your business challenges.

How to Use This Book

This book is designed to teach the fundamentals of SQL and working with databases. Readers who have experience using Excel spreadsheets should find this material accessible but still challenging. Individuals who have not worked with Excel may be more challenged. It is helpful to be familiar with concepts used in Excel, such as rows, columns, tables, mathematical expressions (e.g., Excel formulas), and aggregate calculations (e.g., SUM, AVG, MIN, MAX, COUNT). These concepts will still be taught here, but some practical Excel experience will help expedite understanding.

Basic computer literacy is required, and readers should know how to navigate folders and copy/paste files, as well as download and save files from the Web.

As you go through the material, have a computer on hand to practice the examples. While some people can learn by just reading, it is best to practice the material at some point to reinforce the knowledge.

Proficiency comes through repeated use and practice. In your job, it is likely that you will use some SQL functionalities heavily and others not as much. That is OK. It is more important to become proficient in what your job requires, and consult this book (or Google) as a reference when you need answers about an unfamiliar topic.

When working with technology, you are never expected to know everything. As a matter of fact, technology topics are so vast in number it would be impossible. So it is helpful to develop a degree of tunnel vision and learn only enough to fulfill the task at hand. Otherwise, you can get overwhelmed or distracted learning irrelevant topics. Hopefully this book will give you a foundation of knowledge, and afterward you can continue to learn about topics that are pertinent to you.

You are always welcome to reach out to me at *tmnield@outlook.com*, and I will answer any questions to the best of my ability. If you have questions about positioning your career with technical skillsets or have a SQL question, I might be able to help. I hope that this material not only augments your skillset and career opportunities, but also sparks new interests that excite you like it did for me.

Conventions Used in This Book

The following typographical conventions are used in this book:

Italic
> Indicates new terms, URLs, email addresses, filenames, and file extensions.

`Constant width`
> Used for program listings, as well as within paragraphs to refer to program elements such as variable or function names, databases, data types, environment variables, statements, and keywords.

`Constant width bold`
> Shows commands or other text that should be typed literally by the user.

`Constant width italic`
> Shows text that should be replaced with user-supplied values or by values determined by context.

 This element signifies a general note.

Using Code Examples

Supplemental material (code examples, exercises, etc.) is available for download at *https://github.com/thomasnield/oreilly_getting_started_with_sql*.

This book is here to help you get your job done. In general, if example code is offered with this book, you may use it in your programs and documentation. You do not need to contact us for permission unless you're reproducing a significant portion of the code. For example, writing a program that uses several chunks of code from this book does not require permission. Selling or distributing a CD-ROM of examples from O'Reilly books does require permission. Answering a question by citing this book and quoting example code does not require permission. Incorporating a significant amount of example code from this book into your product's documentation does require permission.

We appreciate, but do not require, attribution. An attribution usually includes the title, author, publisher, and ISBN. For example: "*Getting Started with SQL* by Thomas Nield (O'Reilly). Copyright 2016 Thomas Nield, 978-1-4919-3861-4."

If you feel your use of code examples falls outside fair use or the permission given above, feel free to contact us at *permissions@oreilly.com*.

Safari® Books Online

 *Safari Books Online* is an on-demand digital library that delivers expert content in both book and video form from the world's leading authors in technology and business.

Technology professionals, software developers, web designers, and business and creative professionals use Safari Books Online as their primary resource for research, problem solving, learning, and certification training.

Safari Books Online offers a range of plans and pricing for enterprise, government, education, and individuals.

Members have access to thousands of books, training videos, and prepublication manuscripts in one fully searchable database from publishers like O'Reilly Media, Prentice Hall Professional, Addison-Wesley Professional, Microsoft Press, Sams, Que, Peachpit Press, Focal Press, Cisco Press, John Wiley & Sons, Syngress, Morgan Kaufmann, IBM Redbooks, Packt, Adobe Press, FT Press, Apress, Manning, New Riders, McGraw-Hill, Jones & Bartlett, Course Technology, and hundreds more. For more information about Safari Books Online, please visit us online.

How to Contact Us

Please address comments and questions concerning this book to the publisher:

O'Reilly Media, Inc.
1005 Gravenstein Highway North
Sebastopol, CA 95472
800-998-9938 (in the United States or Canada)
707-829-0515 (international or local)
707-829-0104 (fax)

We have a web page for this book, where we list errata, examples, and any additional information. You can access this page at *http://bit.ly/getting-started-with-sql*.

To comment or ask technical questions about this book, send email to *bookquestions@oreilly.com*.

For more information about our books, courses, conferences, and news, see our website at *http://www.oreilly.com*.

Find us on Facebook: *http://facebook.com/oreilly*

Follow us on Twitter: *http://twitter.com/oreillymedia*

Watch us on YouTube: *http://www.youtube.com/oreillymedia*

Acknowledgments

I am blessed to have amazing people surrounding me, and I realize how central they have been in my life and everything I do. If it was not for them, this book would probably not have happened.

First and foremost, I would like to thank my mom and dad. They have given everything to secure my future. I know for a fact that I would not have the opportunities I have today if it was not for them. My dad worked hard to provide a better education for my brothers and me, and my mother always pushed me forward, even when I resisted. She taught me to never settle and always struggle through my limits.

I cannot express enough gratitude toward my leaders, managers, and colleagues at Southwest Airlines Revenue Management. Justin Jones and Timothy Keeney have a warrior spirit and zeal for innovation that few possess. They truly define the leadership and spirit of Southwest Airlines, but more importantly they are good guys. They will always be my friends and they've made it hard to imagine a life without Southwest Airlines.

Robert Haun, Brice Taylor, and Allison Russell continuously work to make our team the forefront of innovation and continuously pursue new ideas, and I am blessed to work in the environment they have helped create. I also have to thank Matt Louis for bringing me on board at Revenue Management, and Steven Barsalou who made me realize how little I really knew about SQL. Steven is the first person who came to mind when I needed a reviewer for this book, and I am grateful he came on board this project.

Then there is the project team I work with every day: Brian Denholm, Paul Zigler, Bridget Green, Todd Randolph, and Chris Solomon. As a team, the feats we pull off never cease to amaze me. Brian is the kind of project manager that can effectively bridge technology and business jargon together, and he will not hesitate to get his hands dirty with SQL and the occasional code review. I want to give a special thanks to Chris Solomon for helping me with everything I do every day. He not only has a rare talent to absorb high volumes of technical knowledge and maintain it in a business perspective, but he is also a nice guy that I am privileged to be friends with. Chris is always a key player in any project, and I was thrilled when he agreed to review this book.

I cannot forget the great people who worked at Southwest Airlines Ground Ops Safety Regulatory Compliance, including Marc Stank, Reuben Miller, Mary Noel Hennes, and everybody else I had the privilege of working with. I interned and contracted with that department a few years back and some of my fondest memories are there. It was there I discovered my passion for technology, and they provided many opportunities for me to pursue that, whether it was throwing together databases or prototyping an iPad app.

When I announced I was publishing this book I did not expect Richard Hipp, the founder and creator of SQLite, to reach out to me. Richard graciously stepped up to be the technical reviewer for this book and it has been a tremendous honor to have him on board. The technology community continues to amaze me, and the fact Richard Hipp joined this project shows how unique and close-knit the community really is.

Shannon Cutt has been my editor at O'Reilly for this book. This is my first book and I was uncertain what the publishing experience would be like. But Shannon made publishing such a pleasant experience that I am eager to write again. Thanks Shannon, you have been awesome!

Last but not least, I want to thank Watermark Church and the volunteers at Careers in Motion for creating the vehicle that made this book happen. I initially wrote this "book" as a public service to help unemployed professionals in the Dallas area. It was at their encouragement that I decided to publish it, and I want to give a special thanks to Martha Garza for her insistence. I have learned remarkable things can happen when you give your time to help others.

CHAPTER 1

Why Learn SQL?

What Is SQL and Why Is It Marketable?

It is an obvious statement that the business landscape is shifting rapidly. A lot of this is enabled by technology and the explosion of business data. Companies are investing vast amounts of capital to gather and warehouse data. But what many business leaders and managers currently struggle with is how to make sense of this data and use it. This is where *SQL*, which stands for *Structured Query Language*, comes in. It provides a means to access and manipulate this data in meaningful ways and provide business insights not possible before.

Businesses are gathering data at exponential rates, and there is an equally growing need for people who know how to analyze and manage it. Stack Overflow, the most active programming community in the world, performed a comprehensive survey on its members in 2015. Apple coding was the most in-demand technology and had an average salary nearing six figures. But SQL came in in fifth place, with a salary that was not far behind. In recent years, data has suddenly become ubiquitous—yet few people know how to access it meaningfully, which has put SQL talent in high demand.

Who Is SQL For?

One misperception about SQL is that it is an IT skill and therefore only applicable to technology (not business) professionals. In the world as it exists today, this is hardly the truth. Businesspeople, managers, IT professionals, and engineers can all reap benefits from learning SQL to better position their careers. SQL can open many career paths because it enables individuals to know their businesses better through the data that is driving them. On the business side, interest in SQL can lead to roles that are analytical, managerial, strategic, and research- or project-based. On the IT front, it can lead to roles in database design, database administration, systems engineering, IT project management, and even software development.

CHAPTER 2

Databases

What Is a Database?

In the broadest definition, a *database* is anything that collects and organizes data. A spreadsheet holding customer bookings is a database, and so is a plain-text file containing flight schedule data. Plain-text data itself can be stored in a variety of formats, including XML and CSV.

Professionally, however, when one refers to a "database" they likely are referring to a *relational database management system* (RDBMS). This term may sound technical and intimidating, but an RDBMS is simply a type of database that holds one or more tables that may have relationships to each other.

Exploring Relational Databases

A table should be a familiar concept. It has columns and rows to store data, much like a spreadsheet. These tables can have relationships to each other, such as an ORDER table that refers to a CUSTOMER table for customer information.

For example, suppose we have an ORDER table with a field called CUSTOMER_ID (Figure 2-1).

	ORDER_ID	ORDER_DATE	SHIP_DATE	CUSTOMER_ID	PRODUCT_ID	ORDER_QTY	SHIPPED
1	3	2015-04-20	2015-04-23	3	5	300	false
2	4	2015-04-18	2015-04-22	5	4	375	false
3	1	2015-04-15	2015-04-18	1	1	450	false
4	5	2015-04-17	2015-04-20	3	2	500	false
5	2	2015-04-18	2015-04-21	3	2	600	false

Figure 2-1. An ORDER table with a CUSTOMER_ID

We can reasonably expect there to be another table, maybe called `CUSTOMER` (Figure 2-2), which holds the customer information for each `CUSTOMER_ID`.

CUSTOMER ID	NAME	REGION	STREET ADDRESS	CITY	STATE	ZIP
1	LITE Industrial	Southwest	729 Ravine Way	Irving	TX	75014
2	Rex Tooling Inc	Southwest	6129 Collie Blvd	Dallas	TX	75201
3	Re-Barre Construction	Southwest	9043 Windy Dr	Irving	TX	75032
4	Prairie Construction	Southwest	264 Long Rd	Moore	OK	62104
5	Marsh Lane Metal Works	Southeast	9143 Marsh Ln	Avondale	LA	79782

Figure 2-2. A CUSTOMER table

When we go through the `ORDER` table, we can use the `CUSTOMER_ID` to look up the customer information in the `CUSTOMER` table. This is the fundamental idea behind a "relational database," where tables may have fields that point to information in other tables. This concept may sound familiar if you've used VLOOKUP in Excel to retrieve information in one sheet from another sheet in a workbook.

Why Separate Tables?

But why are these tables separated and designed this way? The motivation is *normalization*, which is separating the different types of data into their own tables rather than putting them in one table. If we had all information in a single table, it would be redundant, bloated, and very difficult to maintain. Imagine if we stored customer information in the `ORDER` table. Figure 2-3 shows what it would look like.

	NAME	REGION	STREET ADDRESS	CITY	STATE	ZIP	ORDER ID	ORDER DATE	SHIP DATE	ORDER QTY	SHIPPED
1	LITE Industrial	Southwest	729 Ravine Way	Irving	TX	75014	1	2015-04-15	2015-04-18	450	false
2	Re-Barre Construction	Southwest	9043 Windy Dr	Irving	TX	75032	2	2015-04-18	2015-04-21	600	false
3	Re-Barre Construction	Southwest	9043 Windy Dr	Irving	TX	75032	3	2015-04-20	2015-04-23	300	false
4	Marsh Lane Metal Works	Southeast	9143 Marsh Ln	Avondale	LA	79782	4	2015-04-18	2015-04-22	375	false
5	Re-Barre Construction	Southwest	9043 Windy Dr	Irving	TX	75032	5	2015-04-17	2015-04-20	500	false

Figure 2-3. A table that is not normalized

Notice that for the Re-Barre Construction orders someone had to populate the customer information three times for all three orders (the name, region, street address, city, state, and zip). This is very redundant, takes up unnecessary storage space, and is difficult to maintain. Imagine if a customer had an address change and you had to update all the orders to reflect that. This is why it is better to separate `CUSTOMERS` and `ORDERS` into two separate tables. If you need to change a customer's address, you only need to change one record in the `CUSTOMER` table (Figure 2-4).

	CUSTOMER ID	NAME	REGION	STREET ADDRESS	CITY	STATE	ZIP
1	1	LITE Industrial	Southwest	729 Ravine Way	Irving	TX	75014
2	2	Rex Tooling Inc	Southwest	6129 Collie Blvd	Dallas	TX	75201
3	3	Re-Barre Construction	Southwest	10917 Long Way Rd	Irving	TX	75032
4	4	Prairie Construction	Southwest	264 Long Rd	Moore	OK	62104
5	5	Marsh Lane Metal Works	Southeast	9143 Marsh Ln	Avondale	LA	79782

Figure 2-4. A normalized table

We will explore table relationships again in Chapter 8, and learn how to use the JOIN operator to merge tables in a query so the customer information can be viewed alongside the order.

Choosing a Database Solution

Relational databases and SQL are not proprietary. However, there are several companies and communities that have developed their own relational database software, all of which use tables and leverage SQL. Some database solutions are lightweight and simple, storing data in a single file accessible to a small number of users. Other database solutions are massive and run on a server, supporting thousands of users and applications simultaneously. Some database solutions are free and open source, while others require commercial licenses.

For the sake of practicality, we will divide database solutions into two categories: *lightweight* and *centralized*. These are not necessarily the industry vernacular, but they will help clarify the distinction.

Lightweight Databases

If you are seeking a simple solution for one user or a small number of users (e.g., your coworkers), a lightweight database is a good place to start. Lightweight databases have little to no overhead, meaning they have no servers and are very nimble. Databases are typically stored in a file you can share with others, although it starts to break down when multiple people make edits to the file simultaneously. When you run into this problem, you may want to consider migrating to a centralized database.

The two most common lightweight databases are SQLite and Microsoft Access. SQLite is what we will use in this book. It is free, lightweight, and intuitive to use. It is used in most of the devices we touch and can be found in smartphones, satellites, aircraft, and car systems. It has virtually no size limitation and is ideal for environments where it is not used by more than one person (or at most a few people). Among many other uses, SQLite is ideal to learn SQL due to its ease of installation and simplicity.

Microsoft Access has been around for a while and is inferior to SQLite in terms of scalability and performance. But it is heavily used in business environments and worth being familiar with. It has many visual tools for writing queries without using SQL, as well as visual form designers and macro abilities. There are many jobs available to take ownership of Microsoft Access databases and maintain them, as well as migrating them to better database platforms such as MySQL.

Centralized Databases

If you expect tens, hundreds, or thousands of users and applications to use a database simultaneously, lightweight databases are not going to cut it. You need a centralized database that runs on a server and handles a high volume of traffic efficiently. There is a wide array of centralized database solutions to choose from, including the following:

- MySQL
- Microsoft SQL Server
- Oracle
- PostgreSQL
- Teradata
- IBM DB2
- MariaDB

You can install some of these solutions on any computer and turn that computer into a *server*. You can then connect users' computers (also known as *clients*) to the server so they can access the data. The client can send a SQL statement requesting specific data, and the server processes the request and returns the answer. This is a classic *client–server setup*. The client requests something, and the server gives it.

While you can turn any MacBook or cheap PC into a MySQL server, larger traffic volumes require more specialized computers (called *server computers*) optimized for server tasks. These are typically maintained by an IT department whose members administrate and control databases formally deemed critical to the business.

 Do not be confused by the term "SQL" being used to brand database platforms such as MySQL, Microsoft SQL Server, and SQLite. SQL is the universal language to work with data on all these platforms. They merely used "SQL" in their names for marketing.

As you enter a workplace, chances are an existing centralized database might exist with information you need, and you will need to request access to it. While we will not be covering centralized databases in this book, the experience between different database solutions should largely be the same. Across all database solutions, you use

SQL to interact with tables in a pretty uniform way, and even the SQL editor tools are somewhat similar. Each solution may have nuances to its implementation of SQL, such as date functionalities, but everything in this book should be universally applicable.

If you ever do need to create a centralized database solution, I would highly recommend MySQL. It is open source, free to use, and straightforward to install and set up. It is used by Facebook, Google, eBay, Twitter, and hundreds of other Silicon Valley companies.

With a conceptual understanding of databases, we can now start working with them. Although we will use SQLite in this book, keep in mind it uses SQL, so the knowledge you gain is applicable to all database platforms.

CHAPTER 3

SQLite

What Is SQLite?

As discussed in the previous chapter, there are many places to put data. But oftentimes we want a quick, easy place to put data without all the hassle of a client–server setup. We want to store data in a simple file and edit it just as easily as a Word document. This is an optimal situation to use SQLite.

SQLite is the most widely distributed database in the world. It is put on iPhones, iPads, Android devices, Windows phones, thermostats, car consoles, satellites, and many other modern devices that need to store and retrieve data easily. It is used heavily in the Windows 10 operating system as well as the Airbus A350 XWB aircraft. It excels where simplicity and low overhead is needed. It is also great for prototyping business databases.

But every technology has a trade-off. Because it has no server managing access to it, it fails in multiuser environments where multiple people can simultaneously edit the SQLite file. Still, for our training purposes, SQLite is perfect.

SQLiteStudio

There are many SQL editors you can use to work with a SQLite database. I strongly recommend using SQLiteStudio, as it is intuitive and makes it easy to explore and manage a database. We are going to use that application in this book. You can download it at *http://sqlitestudio.pl/?act=download*. Be sure to choose Windows, Mac, or Linux for your respective OS. Then open the downloaded folder and copy it to a location of your choice. No installation is needed. To start SQLiteStudio, double-click *SQLiteStudio.exe* (Figure 3-1). You can also create a shortcut on your desktop so you can easily launch the application in the future.

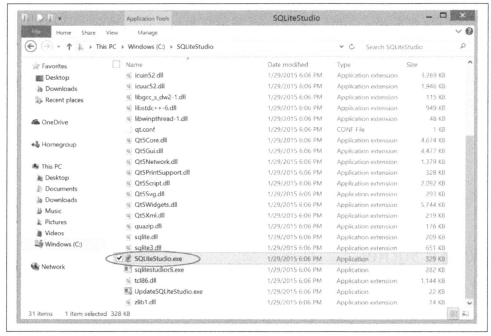

Figure 3-1. The SQLiteStudio folder

Note that SQLiteStudio is an independent, third-party program not associated with SQLite or its developers. SQLite is a database engine built by Richard Hipp and a talented team of programmers. SQLiteStudio merely takes this engine and wraps a nice user interface around it. Therefore, if you ever have issues with SQLiteStudio, you should contact the SQLiteStudio team, not the SQLite team.

Importing and Navigating Databases

When you first start SQLiteStudio, you will probably see a dashboard with no content (Figure 3-2). The left pane is the database navigator, and the gray area on the right is the SQL work area where you will write SQL against the databases.

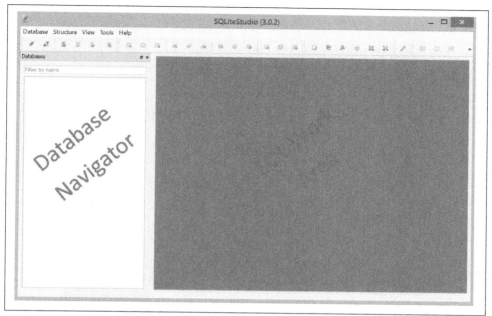

Figure 3-2. The SQLiteStudio dashboard

Let's get some databases into SQLiteStudio. Some SQLite database samples used in this book are provided at *http://bit.ly/1TLw1Gr*.

Download the databases by clicking the Download ZIP button and copy the contents to a folder of your choice. You will probably want to dedicate this folder to all the databases you will work with in this book.

After downloading the databases, navigate in the top menu to Database → Add a Database (Figure 3-3).

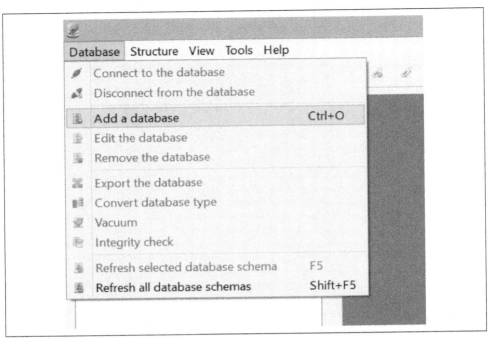

Figure 3-3. Adding a database

You will come to a dialog box prompting for a database file. Click the yellow folder icon to select a database file and import it (Figure 3-4).

Figure 3-4. Opening a database

Browse for the folder with the saved databases, and double-click the *rexon_metals.db* database file to load it into SQLiteStudio (Figure 3-5).

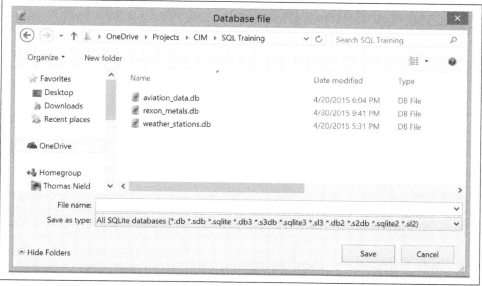

Figure 3-5. Browsing and opening database files

You will now see `rexon_metals` added to the database navigator (Figure 3-6). Double-click on it to see its contents, which include three tables and two views. Take some time to poke around and explore this database in the navigator.

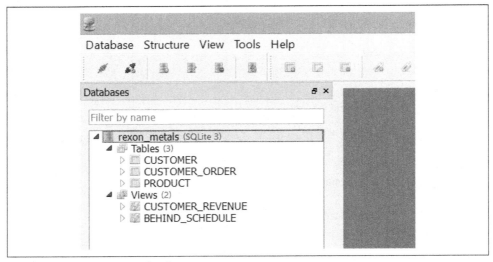

Figure 3-6. Navigating a database

Notice you can click the arrows to get more detailed information on different database objects, such as tables (Figure 3-7). For example, clicking the arrow for the `CUSTOMER` table can reveal information such as the columns it contains.

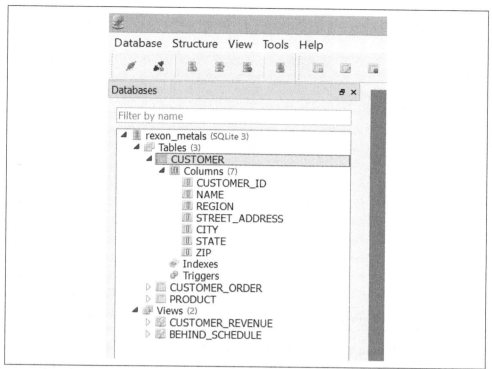

Figure 3-7. Expanding a table to see columns

You may be wondering what "views" are. Do not worry about them for now. They are basically prebuilt SQL queries that are used so frequently, they are conveniently stored in the database.

If you double-click the CUSTOMER table itself, a new window will pop out in the work area holding all kinds of information about the table (Figure 3-8). It initially opens on the Structure tab, which provides detailed information about each column. At the moment, the only detail you need to be concerned with is the data type for each column.

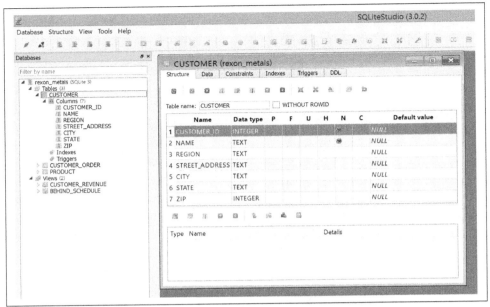

Figure 3-8. Each column in a table has a data type, such as integer or text

The CUSTOMER_ID and ZIP fields are stored as INTEGER, which is the data type for a whole (nondecimal) number. This means these fields should only hold INTEGER values. The rest of the columns are stored as TEXT. There are other data types that could be used, such as DATETIME, BOOLEAN (true/false), and DECIMAL, which are not used in this particular table.

For now, if you understand the concept of data types, then that is all you need to observe in the Structure tab. We will explore table design in detail when we create our own tables later.

Click the Data tab, and you will actually see the data in the table itself (Figure 3-9). There are only five records (or rows) in this table, but SQLite could hold millions if it needed to. You can also conveniently edit the values in this table (without using SQL) by simply double-clicking and editing a cell, and then clicking the green checkmark to save it.

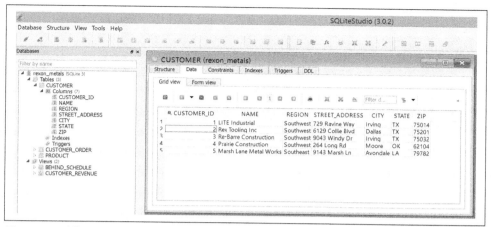

Figure 3-9. The CUSTOMER table

Take some time and get familiar with SQLiteStudio. As soon as you are satisfied that you've poked around enough, close all the windows in the work area. Then, in the top menu, navigate to Tools→Open SQL Editor. While we've discovered that SQLiteStudio provides many ways to view and manipulate data without using any SQL, it does not come close to the flexibility and power that SQL offers.

Now that we know our tables and what we are working with, writing SQL will be somewhat more intuitive. It is difficult to query databases without knowing the tables in them first.

CHAPTER 4

SELECT

When working with databases and SQL, the most common task is to request data from one or more tables and display it. The SELECT statement accomplishes this. But the SELECT can do far more than simply retrieve and display data. As we will learn in coming chapters, we can transform this data in meaningful ways and build powerful summaries from millions of records.

But first, we will learn how to SELECT columns from a single table as well as compose expressions in them.

Retrieving Data with SQL

If you have not done so already, click on Tools→Open SQL Editor in the top menu, and make sure the rexon_metals database is open, as mentioned in the previous chapter. Your SQLiteStudio workspace should look something like Figure 4-1. Notice that the SQL workspace is now divided into two panes, a SQL Editor pane and a Query Results pane.

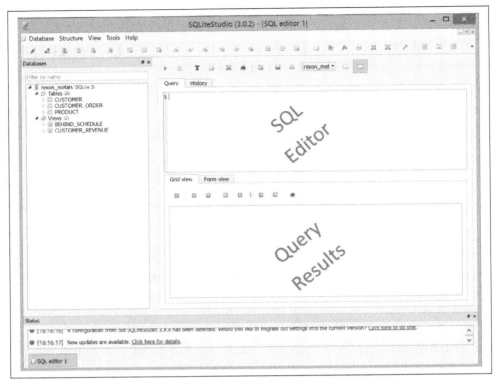

Figure 4-1. The SQL workspace

The SQL Editor pane is where you will write your SQL, and the Query Results pane will display the results of your SQL.

Let's write our first SQL statement. The most common SQL operation is a SELECT statement, which pulls data from a table and then displays the results. Click on the SQL Editor pane and write the following statement:

```
SELECT * FROM CUSTOMER;
```

Click the blue triangle button or hit F9 to execute the SQL.

You just ran your first query, and the results should be displayed in the bottom pane (Figure 4-2).

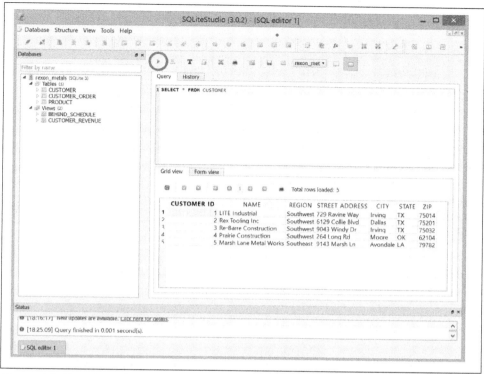

Figure 4-2. Running a SELECT query

Let's break down exactly what happened. A SELECT statement allows you to choose which columns to pull from a table. So the first part of the SQL shown here should be read as "Select all columns," where * is a placeholder to specify all columns:

SELECT * FROM CUSTOMER;

And you are getting these columns from the CUSTOMER table:

SELECT * FROM CUSTOMER;

When you execute this SELECT statement, it brings back all the columns from the CUSTOMER table and displays them to you (Figure 4-3).

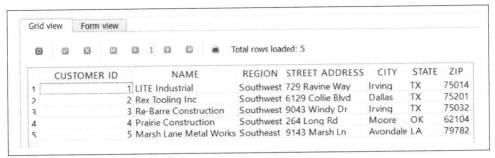

Figure 4-3. Selecting all records from the CUSTOMER table

You do not have to pull all columns in a SELECT statement. You can also pick and choose only the columns you are interested in. The following query will only pull the CUSTOMER_ID and NAME columns:

```
SELECT CUSTOMER_ID, NAME FROM CUSTOMER;
```

And the output will only display those two columns (Figure 4-4).

Figure 4-4. Selecting only two columns from a table

 A single SQL statement can optionally end with a semicolon (;), as shown in the previous examples. However, the semicolon is necessary to run multiple SQL statements at once, which is helpful when writing data, as covered in Chapter 10.

Being able to pick and choose columns may not seem interesting at the moment, but it allows us to hone in on what we are interested in. Reducing scope to just certain columns will assist with GROUP BY aggregation tasks as well, as we'll see in Chapter 6.

Expressions in SELECT Statements

The SELECT statement can do far more than simply select columns. You can also do calculations on one or more columns and include them in your query result.

Let's work with another table called PRODUCT. First, do a SELECT all to see the data (Figure 4-5):

```
SELECT * FROM PRODUCT;
```

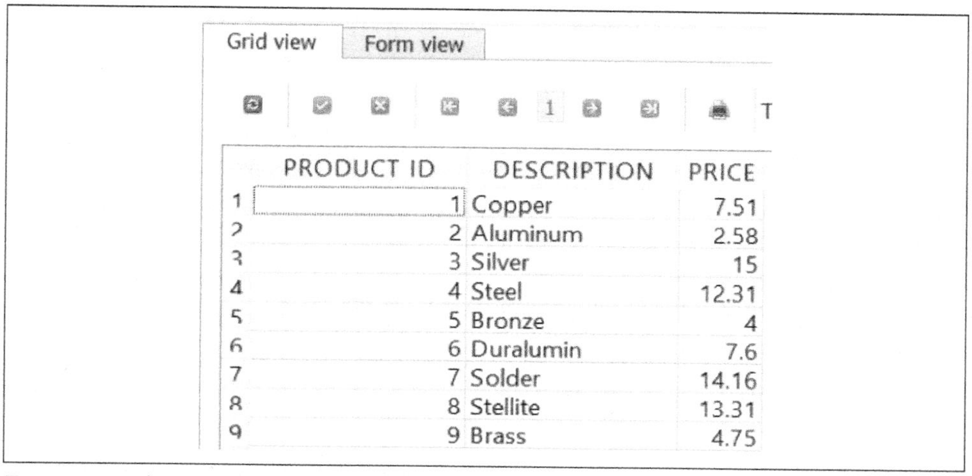

PRODUCT ID	DESCRIPTION	PRICE
1	Copper	7.51
2	Aluminum	2.58
3	Silver	15
4	Steel	12.31
5	Bronze	4
6	Duralumin	7.6
7	Solder	14.16
8	Stellite	13.31
9	Brass	4.75

Figure 4-5. The PRODUCT table

Suppose we wanted to generate a calculated column called TAXED_PRICE that is 7% higher than PRICE. We could use a SELECT query to dynamically calculate this for us (Figure 4-6):

```
SELECT
PRODUCT_ID,
DESCRIPTION,
PRICE,
PRICE * 1.07 AS TAXED_PRICE
FROM PRODUCT;
```

	PRODUCT ID	DESCRIPTION	PRICE	TAXED PRICE
1	1	Copper	7.51	8.0357
2	2	Aluminum	2.58	2.7606
3	3	Silver	15	16.05
4	4	Steel	12.31	13.1717
5	5	Bronze	4	4.28
6	6	Duralumin	7.6	8.132
7	7	Solder	14.16	15.1512
8	8	Stellite	13.31	14.2417
9	9	Brass	4.75	5.0825

Grid view / Form view — Total rows loaded: 9

Figure 4-6. Using expressions to calculate a TAXED_PRICE column

Notice in the SELECT statement that we can spread our SQL across multiple lines to make it more legible. The software will ignore extraneous whitespace and separate lines, so we can use them to make our SQL easier to read.

Notice how the TAXED_PRICE column was dynamically calculated in the SELECT query. This column is not stored in the table, but rather calculated and displayed to us every time we run this query. This is a powerful feature of SQL, which allows us to keep the stored data simple and use queries to layer calculations on top of it.

Let's take a look at our TAXED_PRICE column and break down how it was created. We first see the PRICE is multiplied by 1.07 to calculate the taxed amount. We generate this TAXED_PRICE value for every record:

```
SELECT
PRODUCT_ID,
DESCRIPTION,
PRICE,
PRICE * 1.07 AS TAXED_PRICE
FROM PRODUCT
```

Notice too that we gave this calculated value a name using an AS statement (this is known as an *alias*):

```
SELECT
PRODUCT_ID,
DESCRIPTION,
PRICE,
PRICE * 1.07 AS TAXED_PRICE
FROM PRODUCT
```

We can use aliases to give names to expressions. We can also use aliases to apply a new name to an existing column within the query. For example, we can alias the PRICE column to UNTAXED_PRICE (Figure 4-7). This does not actually change the name of the column in the table, but it gives it a new name within the scope of our SELECT statement:

```
SELECT
PRODUCT_ID,
DESCRIPTION,
PRICE AS UNTAXED_PRICE,
PRICE * 1.07 AS TAXED_PRICE
FROM PRODUCT
```

Grid view	Form view			

Total rows loaded: 9

	PRODUCT ID	DESCRIPTION	UNTAXED PRICE	TAXED PRICE
1	1	Copper	7.51	8.0357
2	2	Aluminum	2.58	2.7606
3	3	Silver	15	16.05
4	4	Steel	12.31	13.1717
5	5	Bronze	4	4.28
6	6	Duralumin	7.6	8.132
7	7	Solder	14.16	15.1512
8	8	Stellite	13.31	14.2417
9	9	Brass	4.75	5.0825

Figure 4-7. Aliasing the PRICE column to UNTAXED_PRICE

When giving names to anything in SQL (whether it is an alias, a column name, a table name, or any other entity), always use an underscore (_) as a placeholder for spaces. You will run into errors otherwise.

If we were to distribute the results of this SQL statement as a report to our workplace, we would probably want to touch up the rounding on the TAXED_PRICE. Having more than two decimal places may not be desirable. Every database platform has built-in *functions* to assist with these kinds of operations, and SQLite provides a `round()` function that accepts two arguments in parentheses separated by a comma: the number to be rounded, and the number of decimal places to round to. To round the `TAXED_PRICE` to two decimal places, we can pass the multiplication expression `PRICE * 1.07` as the first argument, and a 2 as the second:

```
SELECT
PRODUCT_ID,
DESCRIPTION,
PRICE,
round(PRICE * 1.07, 2) AS TAXED_PRICE
FROM PRODUCT;
```

Run the statement and you will notice it rounds the `TAXED_PRICE`, which displays much more nicely with two decimal places (Figure 4-8).

	PRODUCT ID	DESCRIPTION	UNTAXED PRICE	TAXED PRICE
1	1	Copper	7.51	8.04
2	2	Aluminum	2.58	2.76
3	3	Silver	15	16.05
4	4	Steel	12.31	13.17
5	5	Bronze	4	4.28
6	6	Duralumin	7.6	8.13
7	7	Solder	14.16	15.15
8	8	Stellite	13.31	14.24
9	9	Brass	4.75	5.08

Figure 4-8. Using the round() function to limit decimal places for TAXED_PRICE

Here is a short summary of the mathematical operators you can use in SQL (we will see these used throughout the book):

Operator	Description	Example
+	Adds two numbers	STOCK + NEW_SHIPMENT
-	Subtracts two numbers	STOCK - DEFECTS
*	Multiplies two numbers	PRICE * 1.07
/	Divides two numbers	STOCK / PALLET_SIZE
%	Divides two numbers, but returns the remainder	STOCK % PALLET_SIZE

Text Concatenation

Expressions do not have to work only with numbers. You can also use expressions with text and other data types. A helpful operator to use with text is *concatenation*, which merges two or more pieces of data together. The concatenate operator is specified by a double pipe (||), and you put the data values to concatenate on both sides of it.

For instance, you can concatenate the CITY and STATE fields from the CUSTOMER table as well as put a comma and space between them to create a LOCATION value (Figure 4-9):

```
SELECT NAME,
CITY || ', ' || STATE AS LOCATION
FROM CUSTOMER;
```

	NAME	LOCATION
1	LITE Industrial	Irving, TX
2	Rex Tooling Inc	Dallas, TX
3	Re-Barre Construction	Irving, TX
4	Prairie Construction	Moore, OK
5	Marsh Lane Metal Works	Avondale, LA

Figure 4-9. Concatenating CITY and STATE

You can even concatenate several fields into a single SHIP_ADDRESS value (Figure 4-10):

```
SELECT NAME,
STREET_ADDRESS || ' ' || CITY || ', ' || STATE || ' ' || ZIP AS SHIP_ADDRESS
FROM CUSTOMER;
```

NAME	SHIP_ADDRESS
LITE Industrial	729 Ravine Way Irving, TX 75014
Rex Tooling Inc	6129 Collie Blvd Dallas, TX 75201
Re-Barre Construction	9043 Windy Dr Irving, TX 75032
Prairie Construction	264 Long Rd Moore, OK 62104
Marsh Lane Metal Works	9143 Marsh Ln Avondale, LA 79782

Figure 4-10. Concatenating several fields to create a SHIP_ADDRESS

Concatenation should work with any data type (numbers, dates, etc.) and treat it as text when merging. The ZIP field shown here is a number, but it was implicitly converted to text during concatenation.

More text operations will be covered in the next chapter, but concatenation is definitely an important one.

 Many database platforms use double pipes (||) to concatenate, but MySQL and some others require using a CONCAT() function.

Summary

In this chapter, we covered how to use the SELECT statement, the most common SQL operation. It retrieves and transforms data from a table without affecting the table itself. We also learned how to select columns and write expressions. Within expressions, we can use operators and functions to do tasks such as rounding, math, and concatenation.

In the next chapter, we will learn about the WHERE statement, which will allow us to filter records based on criteria we specify.

CHAPTER 5

WHERE

Over the next few chapters, we will be adding more functionalities to the SELECT statement. A very common task when working with data is filtering for records based on criteria, which can be done with a WHERE statement.

We will be learning more functions and using them in the WHERE clause, but we can also use them in SELECT statements, as discussed in the previous chapter. For the most part, expressions and functions can be used in any part of a SQL statement.

Filtering Records

We are going to open another database called weather_stations. Add this database to your database navigator (refer to Chapter 3 if you've forgotten how to do this). Double-click on the database and you will see there is a single table called STA TION_DATA. This contains weather-related sample data gathered from various weather stations.

Execute a SELECT on all columns to see the data inside:

```
SELECT * FROM station_data;
```

There is a lot of data here: about 28,000 records (Figure 5-1). We are not going to glean a lot of interesting information by scrolling through these records one by one. We will need to learn some more SQL features to morph this data into something meaningful. We will start by learning the WHERE statement, which we can use to filter down records based on a criterion.

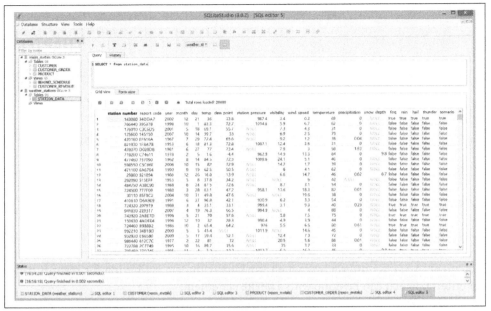

Figure 5-1. The weather_stations database

Table names and columns can be defined in uppercase or lowercase. SQL commands such as SELECT, FROM, and WHERE can be uppercase or lowercase as well.

Using WHERE on Numbers

Let's say we are interested in **station_data** records for only the year 2010. Using a WHERE is pretty straightforward for a simple criterion like this. With this query, you should only get back records where the **year** field equals **2010** (Figure 5-2):

```
SELECT * FROM station_data
WHERE year = 2010;
```

Total rows loaded: 249

station number	report code	year	month	day	dew point	station pressure	visibility	wind sp
1	719160 BAB974	2010	1	22	-22.8	1014.2	NULL	
2	766870 7C0938	2010	3	22	48	871.2	4.4	
3	134624 11CEA1	2010	2	17	46	NULL	3.4	
4	384010 C67A6C	2010	3	24	14.4	NULL	4	
5	232210 DFDF58	2010	2	25	-7.3	NULL	3	
6	717385 302766	2010	3	14	28.9	NULL	NULL	
7	726375 36C13D	2010	3	6	18.9	NULL	10	
8	710140 7FE84E	2010	4	2	8.7	NULL	NULL	NUL
9	965950 80413C	2010	2	25	75.6	1006.8	3.5	
10	144470 079A10	2010	1	28	34.3	1001.9	7.9	

Figure 5-2. Records for the year 2010

Conversely, you can use != or <> to get everything but 2010. For example:

```
SELECT * FROM station_data
WHERE year != 2010
```

Or:

```
SELECT * FROM station_data
WHERE year <> 2010
```

These two syntaxes do the same thing. SQLite and most platforms now support both. However, Microsoft Access and IBM DB2 only support <>.

We can also qualify inclusive ranges using a BETWEEN statement, as shown here ("inclusive" means that 2005 and 2010 are included in the range):

```
SELECT * FROM station_data
WHERE year BETWEEN 2005 and 2010
```

AND, OR, and IN Statements

A BETWEEN can alternatively be expressed using greater than or equal to and less than or equal to expressions and an AND statement. It is a little more verbose, but it demonstrates we can use two conditions with an AND. In this case, the year must be greater than or equal to 2005 and less than or equal to 2010:

```
SELECT * FROM station_data
WHERE year >= 2005 AND year <= 2010
```

If we wanted everything between 2005 and 2010 exclusively—i.e., not including those two years—we would just get rid of the = characters. Only 2006, 2007, 2008, and 2009 would then qualify:

```
SELECT * FROM station_data
WHERE year > 2005 AND year < 2010
```

We also have the option of using OR. In an OR statement, at least one of the criteria must be true for the record to qualify. If we wanted only records with months 3, 6, 9, or 12, we could use an OR to accomplish that:

```
SELECT * FROM station_data
WHERE MONTH = 3
OR MONTH = 6
OR MONTH = 9
OR MONTH = 12
```

This is a little verbose. A more efficient way to accomplish this is using an IN statement to provide valid list of values:

```
SELECT * FROM station_data
WHERE MONTH IN (3,6,9,12)
```

If we wanted everything except 3, 6, 9, and 12, we could use NOT IN:

```
SELECT * FROM station_data
WHERE MONTH NOT IN (3,6,9,12)
```

You can use other math expressions in your WHERE statements too. Earlier, we were trying to filter on months 3, 6, 9, and 12. If you wanted only months divisible by 3 (the "quarter" months), you could use the *modulus operator* (%). The modulus is similar to the division operator (/), but it returns the remainder instead of the quotient. A remainder of 0 means there is no remainder at all, so you can leverage this logic by looking for a remainder of 0 with modulus 3.

In English, this means "give me all months where dividing by 3 gives me a remainder of 0":

```
SELECT * FROM station_data
WHERE MONTH % 3 = 0
```

 Oracle does not support the modulus operator. It instead uses the MOD() function.

Using WHERE on Text

We've covered several examples of how to qualify number fields in WHERE statements. The rules for qualifying text fields follow the same structure, although there are subtle differences. You can use =, AND, OR, and IN statements with text. However, when using text, you must wrap *literals* (or text values you specify) in single quotes. For example, if you wanted to filter for a specific report_code, you could run this query:

```
SELECT * FROM station_data
WHERE report_code = '513A63'
```

Notice that because the `report_code` field is text (not a number), we need to put single quotes around `'513A63'` to qualify it. If we do not do this, the SQL software will get confused and think 513A63 is a column rather than a text value. This will cause an error and the query will fail.

This single-quote rule applies to all text operations, including this `IN` operation:

```
SELECT * FROM station_data
WHERE report_code IN ('513A63','1F8A7B','EF616A')
```

There are other helpful text operations and functions you can use in `WHERE` and `SELECT` statements. For example, the `length()` function will count the number of characters for a given value. So, if we were assigned quality control and needed to ensure every `report_code` was six characters in length, we would want to make sure no records come back when running this query:

```
SELECT * FROM station_data
WHERE length(report_code) != 6
```

Another common operation is to use wildcards with a `LIKE` expression, where `%` is any number of characters and `_` is any single character. Any other character is interpreted literally. So, if you wanted to find all report codes that start with the letter "A," you would run this statement to find "A" followed by any characters:

```
SELECT * FROM station_data
WHERE report_code LIKE 'A%'
```

If you wanted to find all report codes that have a "B" as the first character and a "C" as the third character, you would specify an underscore (_) for the second position, and follow with any number of characters after the "C":

```
SELECT * FROM station_data
WHERE report_code LIKE 'B_C%'
```

 Do not be confused by the `%` being used for two different purposes. Earlier we used it to perform a modulus operation, but in a `LIKE` statement it is a wildcard in a text pattern. Like some other symbols and characters in SQL, the context in which it is used defines its functionality.

There are many other handy text functions, such as `INSTR`, `SUBSTR`, and `REPLACE`. In the interest of brevity, we will stop covering text functions here, but you can refer to "APPENDIX A6 – Common Core Functions" on page 103 and "APPENDIX A8 – Date and Time Functions" on page 104 for more coverage on these functions.

Text functions such as LIKE, SUBSTR, and INSTR can start to become tedious and verbose when qualifying complex text patterns. I highly recommend researching *regular expressions* when you find yourself experiencing this. They are not beginner material, but they are handy once you hit that intermediate need.

Using WHERE on Booleans

Booleans are true/false values. In the database world, typically false is expressed as 0 and true is expressed as 1. Some database platforms (like MySQL) allow you to implicitly use the words true and false to qualify, as shown here:

```
SELECT * FROM station_data
WHERE tornado = true AND hail = true;
```

SQLite, however, does not support this. It expects you to explicitly use 1 for true and 0 for false. If you wanted all records where there was tornado and hail, you would run this statement:

```
SELECT * FROM station_data
WHERE tornado = 1 AND hail = 1;
```

If you are looking for just true values, you do not even have to use the = 1 expression. Because the fields are already Boolean (behind the scenes, every WHERE condition boils down to a Boolean expression), they inherently qualify by themselves. Hence, you can achieve the same results by running the following query:

```
SELECT * FROM station_data
WHERE tornado AND hail;
```

However, qualifying for false conditions needs to be explicit. To get all records with no tornado but with hail, run this query:

```
SELECT * FROM station_data
WHERE tornado = 0 AND hail = 1;
```

You can also use the NOT keyword to qualify tornado as false:

```
SELECT * FROM station_data
WHERE NOT tornado AND hail;
```

Handling NULL

You may have noticed that some columns, such as station_pressure and snow_depth, have *null* values (Figure 5-3). A null is a value that has no value. It is the complete absence of any content. It is a vacuous state. In layman's terms, it is blank.

Total rows loaded: 28000

station number	report code	year	month	day	dew point	station pressure	visibility	wind speed	temperature	precipitation	snow depth
143080	34DDA7	2002	12	21	33.8	987.4	3.4	0.2	69	0	NULL
766440	39537B	1998	10	1	72.7	1014.6	5.9	6.7	62	0	NULL
176010	C3C6D5	2001	5	18	55.7	NULL	7.3	4.3	31	0	NULL
125600	145150	2007	10	14	33	NULL	6.9	2.5	79	0	NULL
470160	EF616A	1967	7	29	65.6	NULL	9.2	1.2	38	0.04	NULL
821930	1F8A7B	1953	6	18	72.8	1007.1	12.4	3.6	31	0	NULL
478070	D028D8	1981	6	27	73.4	NULL	7.9	3	58	1.93	NULL
719200	C74611	1978	2	5	-4.4	962.9	14.9	13.3	84	0	9.8
477460	737090	1962	8	14	72.3	1009.6	24.1	5.1	40	0	NULL
598550	C5C66E	2006	10	15	72.9	NULL	14.2	1.7	39	0	NULL
471100	6A6704	1990	9	19	50.5	NULL	6	4.1	62	0	NULL
29880	921894	1986	12	26	13.9	NULL	6.6	14.7	46	0.02	8.7
292090	515EFF	1953	5	8	34.2	NULL	NULL	6	42	NULL	NULL
484750	A38C90	1988	6	24	72.6	NULL	8.7	3.1	54	0	NULL

Figure 5-3. The station_data table has NULL values

Null values cannot be determined with an =. You need to use the IS NULL or IS NOT NULL statements to identify null values. So, to get all records with no recorded snow_depth, you could run this query:

```
SELECT * FROM station_data
WHERE snow_depth IS NULL;
```

Often, null values are not desirable to have. The station_number column should be designed so it never allows nulls, or else we could have orphan data that belongs to no station. It might make sense to have null values for snow_depth or precipitation, though, not because it was a sunny day (in this case, it is better to record the values as 0), but rather because some stations might not have the necessary instruments to take those measurements. It might be misleading to set those values to 0 (which implies data was recorded), so those measurements should be left null.

This shows that nulls can be ambiguous and it can be difficult to determine their business meaning. It is important that *nullable columns* (columns that are allowed to have null values) have documented what a null value means from a business perspective. Otherwise, nulls should be banned from those table columns.

Do not confuse nulls with empty text, which is two single quotes with nothing in them (i.e., ''). This also applies to whitespace text (i.e., ' '). These will be treated as values and never will be considered null. A null is definitely not the same as 0 either, because 0 is a value, whereas null is an absence of a value.

Nulls can be very annoying to handle when composing WHERE statements. If you wanted to query all records where precipitation is less than 0.5, you could write this statement:

```
SELECT * FROM station_data
WHERE precipitation <= 0.5;
```

But have you considered the null values? What if for this query you wanted nulls to be included? Because null is not 0 or any number, it will not qualify. Nulls rarely qualify with anything and almost always get filtered out in a WHERE unless you explicitly handle them. So you have to use an OR to include nulls:

```
SELECT * FROM station_data
WHERE precipitation IS NULL OR precipitation <= 0.5;
```

A more elegant way of handling null values is to use the coalesce() function, which will turn a possibly null value into a specified default value if it is null. Otherwise, it will leave the value as is. The first argument is the possibly null value, and the second is the value to use if it is null. So if we wanted all nulls to be treated as 0 within our condition, we could coalesce() the precipitation field to convert null to 0:

```
SELECT * FROM station_data
WHERE coalesce(precipitation, 0) <= 0.5;
```

Like any function, a coalesce() can be used in the SELECT statement too, and not just the WHERE. This is helpful if you want to pretty up a report and not have null values displayed, but rather have some placeholder—for example, 0, "N/A" or "None"—which is more meaningful to most people:

```
SELECT report_code, coalesce(precipitation, 0) as rainfall
FROM station_data;
```

Grouping Conditions

When you start chaining AND and OR together, it is good to group them deliberately. You need to make sure that you organize each set of conditions between each OR in a way that groups related conditions. Say you were looking for sleet or snow conditions. For sleet to happen, there must be rain *and* a temperature less than or equal to 32 degrees Fahrenheit. You can test for that sleet condition *or* a snow depth greater than 0, as shown here:

```
SELECT * FROM station_data
WHERE rain = 1 AND temperature <= 32
OR snow_depth > 0;
```

But there is one possible problem here. While this technically works, there is a degree of ambiguity that we were lucky SQLite interpreted correctly. The reason is due to the unclear question of "What conditions belong to the AND and what conditions belong to the OR?" The SQL interpreter could derail quickly and incorrectly interpret that we are looking for rain AND another condition where either the temperature is below 32 OR the snow depth is greater than 0. The semantics are not clear, and in more complicated SQL this could confuse not only people but also the machine.

This is why it is better to explicitly group conditions in parentheses:

```
SELECT * FROM station_data
WHERE (rain = 1 AND temperature <= 32)
OR snow_depth > 0
```

Here, we group up the sleet expression within parentheses so it is calculated as a single unit, and `temperature` is not mixed up with the `OR` operator and accidentally mangled with the `snow_depth`. Grouping with parentheses in `WHERE` statements not only makes the semantics clearer, but also the execution safer. This is much like the order of operations (PEMDAS) you probably remember from your middle school math days. Anything in parentheses gets calculated first. When you start writing complicated `WHERE` conditions, this practice becomes even more critical.

Summary

In this chapter, we learned to effectively filter out records in a `SELECT` statement using a `WHERE` clause. We also leveraged new functions and expression operators that can be used in almost any part of the SQL statement. Finally, we covered how to deliberately and safely chain multiple conditions together in a single `WHERE` statement.

Hopefully SQL is already proving to be useful. You can quickly and easily filter data on very explicit conditions, in a way that is difficult to achieve in everyday tools like Excel.

Despite all we have covered, we have only just gotten started. The next chapter will cover aggregating data, which will add even more value to your SQL repertoire. It is one thing to narrow down your records and filter on specific criteria. It is another to crunch down millions of records into a few that summarize the data.

We covered a few functions in this chapter, but there are dozens more that you can research and use as needed. We will learn a few more throughout this book. "APPENDIX A6 – Common Core Functions" on page 103 and "APPENDIX A8 – Date and Time Functions" on page 104 cover several more of these functions, and you can always see a full list of SQLite functions at *https://www.sqlite.org/lang_corefunc.html*.

CHAPTER 6

GROUP BY and ORDER BY

Aggregating data (also referred to as rolling up, summarizing, or grouping data) is creating some sort of total from a number of records. Sum, min, max, count, and average are common aggregate operations. In SQL you can group these totals on any specified columns, allowing you to control the scope of these aggregations easily.

Grouping Records

First, perform the simplest aggregation: count the number of records in a table. Open the SQL editor and get a count of records for station data:

```
SELECT COUNT(*) AS record_count FROM station_data;
```

The COUNT(*) means to count the records. We can also use this in combination with other SQL operations, like WHERE. To count the number of records where a tornado was present, input the following:

```
SELECT COUNT(*) AS record_count FROM station_data
WHERE tornado = 1;
```

We identified 3,000 records with tornadoes present. But what if we wanted to separate the count by year (Figure 6-1)? We can do that too with this query:

```
SELECT year, COUNT(*) AS record_count FROM station_data
WHERE tornado = 1
GROUP BY year;
```

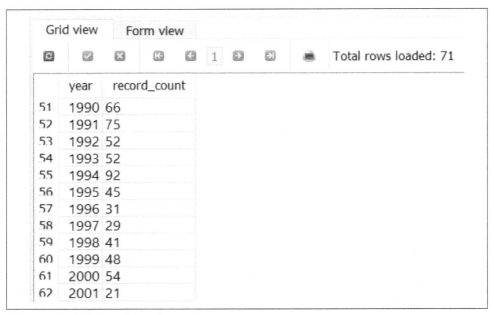

Figure 6-1. Getting a tornado count by year

This data suddenly becomes more meaningful. We now see the tornado sighting count by year. Let's break down this query to see how this happened.

First, we select the year, then we select the COUNT(*) from the records, and we filter only for records where tornado is true:

```
SELECT year, COUNT(*) AS record_count FROM station_data
WHERE tornado = 1
GROUP BY year;
```

However, we also specify that we are *grouping* on year. This is what effectively allows us to count the number of records *by year*. The last line, highlighted in bold, performs this grouping:

```
SELECT year, COUNT(*) AS record_count FROM station_data
WHERE tornado = 1
GROUP BY year;
```

We can slice this data on more than one field. If we wanted a count by year and month, we could group on the month field as well (Figure 6-2):

```
SELECT year, month, COUNT(*) AS record_count FROM station_data
WHERE tornado = 1
GROUP BY year, month
```

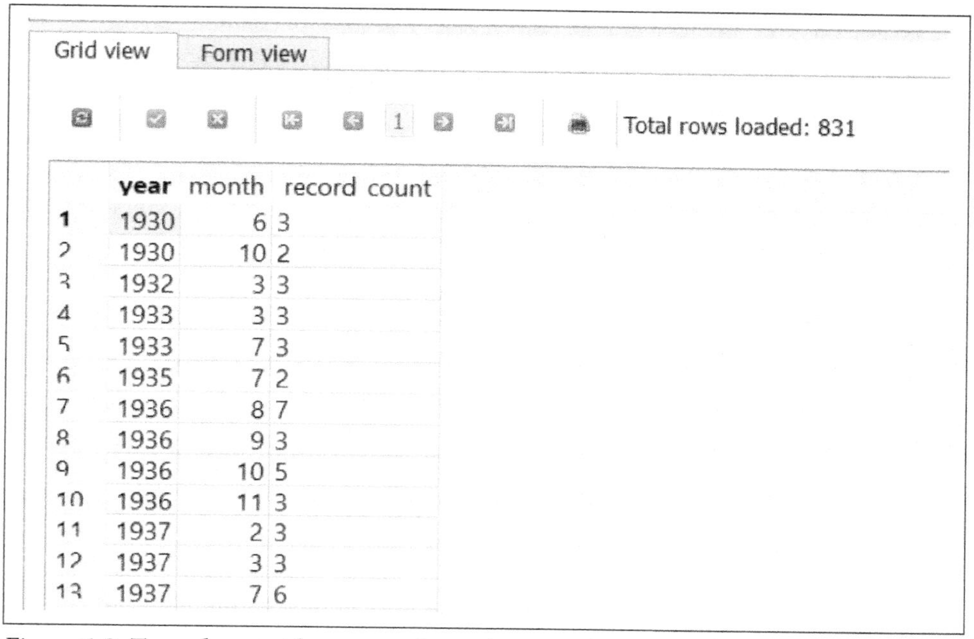

	year	month	record_count
1	1930	6	3
2	1930	10	2
3	1932	3	3
4	1933	3	3
5	1933	7	3
6	1935	7	2
7	1936	8	7
8	1936	9	3
9	1936	10	5
10	1936	11	3
11	1937	2	3
12	1937	3	3
13	1937	7	6

Figure 6-2. Tornado count by year and month

Alternatively, we can use *ordinal positions* instead of specifying the columns in the `GROUP BY`. The ordinal positions correspond to each item's numeric position in the `SELECT` statement. So, instead of writing `GROUP BY year, month`, we could instead make it `GROUP BY 1, 2` (which is especially helpful if our `SELECT` has long column names or expressions, and we do not want to rewrite them in the `GROUP BY`):

```
SELECT year, month, COUNT(*) AS record_count FROM station_data
WHERE tornado = 1
GROUP BY 1, 2
```

Note that not all platforms support ordinal positions. With Oracle and SQL Server, for example, you will have to rewrite the entire column name or expression in the `GROUP BY`.

Ordering Records

Notice that the `month` column is not in a natural sort we would expect. This is a good time to bring up the `ORDER BY` operator, which you can put at the end of a SQL statement (after any `WHERE` and `GROUP BY`). If you wanted to sort by `year`, and then `month`, you could just add this command:

```
SELECT year, month, COUNT(*) AS record_count FROM station_data
WHERE tornado = 1
GROUP BY year, month
ORDER BY year, month
```

However, you are probably more interested in recent data and would like it at the top. By default, sorting is done with the ASC operator, which orders the data in ascending order. If you want to sort in descending order instead, apply the DESC operator to the ordering of year to make more recent records appear at the top of the results:

```
SELECT year, month, COUNT(*) AS record_count FROM station_data
WHERE tornado = 1
GROUP BY year, month
ORDER BY year DESC, month
```

Aggregate Functions

We already used the COUNT(*) function to count records. But there are other aggregation functions, including SUM(), MIN(), MAX(), and AVG(). We can use aggregation functions on a specific column to perform some sort of calculation on it.

But first let's look at another way to use COUNT(). The COUNT() function can be used for a purpose other than simply counting records. If you specify a column instead of an asterisk, it will count the number of non-null values in that column. For instance, we can take a count of snow_depth recordings, which will count the number of non-null values (Figure 6-3):

```
SELECT COUNT(snow_depth) as recorded_snow_depth_count
FROM STATION_DATA
```

Figure 6-3. Count of non-null snow depth recordings

Taking a count of non-null values in a column can be useful, so take note that COUNT() can fulfill that purpose as well when applied to a column.

Aggregate functions such as COUNT(), SUM(), AVG(), MIN(), and MAX() will never include null values in their calculations. Only non-null values will be considered.

Let's move on to other aggregation tasks. If you wanted to find the average temperature for each month since 2000, you could filter for years 2000 and later, group by month, and perform an average on temp (Figure 6-4):

```
SELECT month, AVG(temp) as avg_temp
FROM station_data
WHERE year >= 2000
GROUP BY month
```

	month	avg temp
1	1	41.5558544303798
2	2	38.980631276901
3	3	48.9750626566416
4	4	52.79985163204 74
5	5	58.4553191489361
6	6	64.344536423841
7	7	69.74756302521
8	8	68.0215384615385
9	9	62.632428115016
10	10	56.3823008849557
11	11	47.5029556650247
12	12	41.1165938864629

Total rows loaded: 12

Figure 6-4. Average temperature by month since the year 2000

As always, you can use functions on the aggregated values and perform tasks such as rounding to make them look nicer (Figure 6-5):

```
SELECT month, round(AVG(temp),2) as avg_temp
FROM station_data
WHERE year >= 2000
GROUP BY month
```

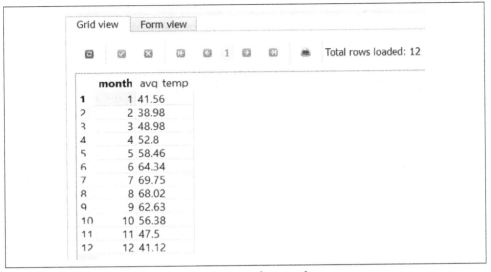

	month	avg temp
1	1	41.56
2	2	38.98
3	3	48.98
4	4	52.8
5	5	58.46
6	6	64.34
7	7	69.75
8	8	68.02
9	9	62.63
10	10	56.38
11	11	47.5
12	12	41.12

Figure 6-5. Rounding the average temperature by month

SUM() is another common aggregate operation. To find the sum of snow depth by year since 2000, run this query:

```
SELECT year, SUM(snow_depth) as total_snow
FROM station_data
WHERE year >= 2000
GROUP BY year
```

There is no limitation on how many aggregate operations you can use in a single query. Here we find the total_snow and total_precipitation for each year since 2000 in a single query, as well as the max_precipitation:

```
SELECT year,
SUM(snow_depth) as total_snow,
SUM(precipitation) as total_precipitation,
MAX(precipitation) as max_precipitation
FROM station_data
WHERE year >= 2000
GROUP BY year
```

It may not be apparent yet, but you can achieve some very specific aggregations by leveraging the WHERE. If you wanted the total precipitation by year only when a tornado was present, you would just have to filter on tornado being true. This will only include tornado-related precipitation in the totals:

```
SELECT year,
SUM(precipitation) as tornado_precipitation
FROM station_data
WHERE tornado = 1
GROUP BY year
```

The HAVING Statement

Suppose you wanted to filter out records based on an aggregated value. While your first instinct might be to use a WHERE statement, this actually will not work because the WHERE filters records, and does not filter aggregations. For example, if you try to use a WHERE to filter results where `total_precipitation` is greater than 30, this will error out:

```
SELECT year,
SUM(precipitation) as total_precipitation
FROM station_data
WHERE total_precipitation > 30
GROUP BY year
```

Why does this not work? You cannot filter on aggregated fields using WHERE. You have to use the HAVING keyword to accomplish this. The way aggregation works is that the software processes record by record, finding which ones it wants to keep based on the WHERE condition. After that, it crunches the records down on the GROUP BY and performs any aggregate functions, such as SUM(). If we wanted to filter on the SUM() value, we would need the filter to take place after it is calculated. This is where HAVING can be applied:

```
SELECT year,
SUM(precipitation) as total_precipitation
FROM station_data
GROUP BY year
HAVING total_precipitation > 30
```

HAVING is the aggregated equivalent to WHERE. The WHERE keyword filters individual records, but HAVING filters aggregations.

Note that some platforms, including Oracle, do not support aliases in the HAVING statement (just like the GROUP BY). This means you must specify the aggregate function again in the HAVING statement. If you were running the preceding query on an Oracle database, you would have to write it like this:

```
SELECT year,
SUM(precipitation) as total_precipitation
FROM station_data
GROUP BY year
HAVING SUM(precipitation) > 30
```

Getting Distinct Records

It is not uncommon to want a set of distinct results from a query. We know there are 28,000 records in our `station_data` table. But suppose we want to get a distinct list of the `station_number` values? If we run this query, we will get duplicates:

```
SELECT station_number FROM station_data
```

If we want a distinct list of station numbers without any duplicates, we can use the `DISTINCT` keyword:

```
SELECT DISTINCT station_number FROM station_data
```

You can also get distinct results for more than one column. If you need the distinct `station_number` and `year` sets, just include both of those columns in the `SELECT` statement:

```
SELECT DISTINCT station_number, year FROM station_data
```

Summary

In this chapter, we learned how to aggregate and sort data using `GROUP BY` and `ORDER BY`. We also leveraged the `SUM()`, `MAX()`, `MIN()`, `AVG()`, and `COUNT()` aggregate functions to crunch thousands of records into a few meaningful totaled records. Because we cannot use `WHERE` to filter aggregated fields, we used the `HAVING` keyword to accomplish that. We also leveraged the `DISTINCT` operator to get distinct results in our queries and eliminate duplicates.

I hope by now you see the flexibility SQL offers to quickly develop meaningful reports based on thousands or millions of records. Before moving on, I would recommend experimenting with everything you've learned so far and trying out the `SELECT`, `WHERE`, and `GROUP BY` in your queries. Ask yourself business questions such as "Has the temperature been getting warmer every January for the past 20 years?" or "How many times has hail been present versus not present during a tornado?" Try to create SQL queries on the weather data to answer these questions.

Get comfortable with what you have learned so far, but do not fret about memorizing every SQL functionality. That will come with time as you repeatedly use and practice SQL. You'll gain more knowledge in the coming chapters, and it's OK to refer to Google or this guide if you forget how to compose things.

 You can get the short, complete list of SQLite aggregate functions in "APPENDIX A7 – Aggregate Functions" on page 104 or at *https://www.sqlite.org/lang_aggfunc.html*.

CHAPTER 7

CASE Statements

We are almost ready to learn the truly defining feature of SQL, the JOIN operator. But before we do that, we should spend a short chapter covering a very handy operator called CASE. This command allows us to swap a column value for another value based on one or more conditions.

The CASE Statement

A CASE statement allows us to map one or more conditions to a corresponding value for each condition. You start a CASE statement with the word CASE and conclude it with an END. Between those keywords, you specify each condition with a WHEN *[condition]* THEN *[value]*, where the *[condition]* and the corresponding *[value]* are supplied by you. After specifying the condition–value pairs, you can have a catch-all value to default to if none of the conditions were met, which is specified in the ELSE. For example, we could categorize wind_speed into wind_severity categories (Figure 7-1), where any speed greater than 40 is 'HIGH', 30 to 40 is 'MODERATE', and anything less is 'LOW':

```
SELECT report_code, year, month, day, wind_speed,

CASE
    WHEN wind_speed >= 40 THEN 'HIGH'
    WHEN wind_speed >= 30 AND wind_speed < 40 THEN 'MODERATE'
    ELSE 'LOW'
END as wind_severity

FROM station_data
```

	report_code	year	month	day	wind_speed	🔍 wind_severity
22	6757E5	1992	10	9	43.9	HIGH
23	E681EA	1984	2	10	44.9	HIGH
24	F7D723	2003	5	23	45.3	HIGH
25	B6A78C	1973	7	17	42.3	HIGH
26	1C8A2A	1998	11	21	50	HIGH
27	34DDA7	2002	12	21	0.2	LOW
28	39537B	1998	10	1	6.7	LOW
29	C3C6D5	2001	5	18	4.3	LOW
30	145150	2007	10	14	2.5	LOW
31	EF616A	1967	7	29	1.2	LOW

Figure 7-1. Categorizing wind severity into HIGH, MODERATE, and LOW

We can actually omit the AND wind_speed < 40 condition. Here is why: the machine reads a CASE statement from top to bottom, and the first condition it finds true is the one it uses (and it will stop evaluating subsequent conditions). So if we have a record with a wind_speed of 43, we can be certain it will be evaluated as 'HIGH'. Although it is greater than 30, it will not be assigned 'MODERATE' because it will not get to that point. Knowing this allows us to create a slightly more efficient query:

```
SELECT report_code, year, month, day, wind_speed,

CASE
    WHEN wind_speed >= 40 THEN 'HIGH'
    WHEN wind_speed >= 30 THEN 'MODERATE'
    ELSE 'LOW'
END as wind_severity

FROM station_data
```

Grouping CASE Statements

When you create CASE statements and group them, you can create some very powerful transformations. Converting values based on one or more conditions before aggregating them gives us even more possibilities to slice data in interesting ways. Elaborating on our previous example, we can group on year and wind_severity and get a count of records for each one as shown here (also notice we use GROUP BY with ordinal positions so we do not have to rewrite the wind_severity case expression in the GROUP BY):

```
SELECT year,

CASE
    WHEN wind_speed >= 40 THEN 'HIGH'
    WHEN wind_speed >= 30 THEN 'MODERATE'
    ELSE 'LOW'
END as wind_severity,

COUNT(*) as record_count

FROM station_data
GROUP BY 1, 2
```

The "Zero/Null" CASE Trick

You can do some clever tricks with the CASE statement. One simple but helpful pattern is the "zero/null" CASE trick. This allows you to apply different "filters" for different aggregate values, all in a single SELECT query. You could never accomplish this in a WHERE because the WHERE applies a filter to everything. But you can use a CASE to create a different filter condition for each aggregate value.

Say you wanted to aggregate precipitation into two sums, tornado_precipitation and non_tornado_precipitation, and GROUP BY year and month. The logic is primarily dependent on two fields: precipitation and tornado. But how exactly do you code this?

If you give it some thought, you will realize you cannot do this with a WHERE statement unless you do two separate queries (one for tornado being true and the other false):

Tornado precipitation

```
SELECT year, month,
SUM(precipitation) as tornado_precipitation
FROM station_data
WHERE tornado = 1
GROUP BY year, month
```

Non-tornado precipitation

```
SELECT year, month,
SUM(precipitation) as non_tornado_precipitation
FROM station_data
WHERE tornado = 0
GROUP BY year, month
```

But it is possible to do this in a single query using a CASE statement. You can move the tornado conditions from the WHERE to a CASE, and make the value 0 if the condition is false. Then you can SUM those CASE statements (Figure 7-2):

```
SELECT year, month,

SUM(CASE WHEN tornado = 1 THEN precipitation ELSE 0 END) as tornado_precipitation,

SUM(CASE WHEN tornado = 0 THEN precipitation ELSE 0 END) as
    non_tornado_precipitation

FROM station_data
GROUP BY year, month
```

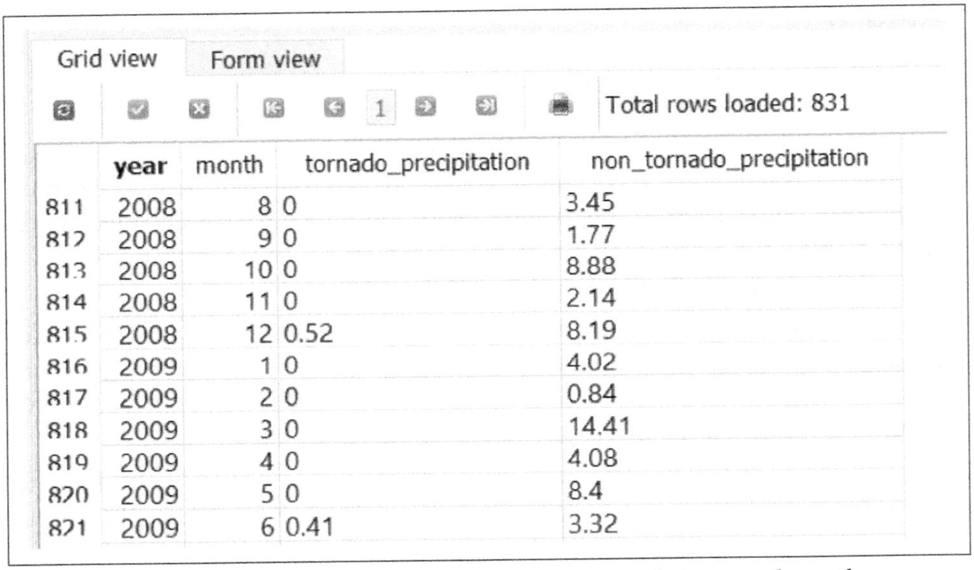

	year	month	tornado_precipitation	non_tornado_precipitation
811	2008	8	0	3.45
812	2008	9	0	1.77
813	2008	10	0	8.88
814	2008	11	0	2.14
815	2008	12	0.52	8.19
816	2009	1	0	4.02
817	2009	2	0	0.84
818	2009	3	0	14.41
819	2009	4	0	4.08
820	2009	5	0	8.4
821	2009	6	0.41	3.32

Grid view Form view — Total rows loaded: 831

Figure 7-2. Getting tornado and non-tornado precipitation by year and month

The CASE statement can do an impressive amount of work, especially in complex aggregation tasks. By leveraging a condition to make a value 0 if the condition is not met, we effectively ignore that value and exclude it from the SUM (because adding 0 has no impact).

You could also do this with MIN or MAX operations, and use a null instead of 0 to make sure values with certain conditions are never considered. You can find the maximum precipitation when tornadoes were present and when they were not (Figure 7-3) as follows:

```
SELECT year,

MAX(CASE WHEN tornado = 0 THEN precipitation ELSE NULL END) as
    max_non_tornado_precipitation,

MAX(CASE WHEN tornado = 1 THEN precipitation ELSE NULL END) as
    max_tornado_precipitation

FROM station_data
GROUP BY year
```

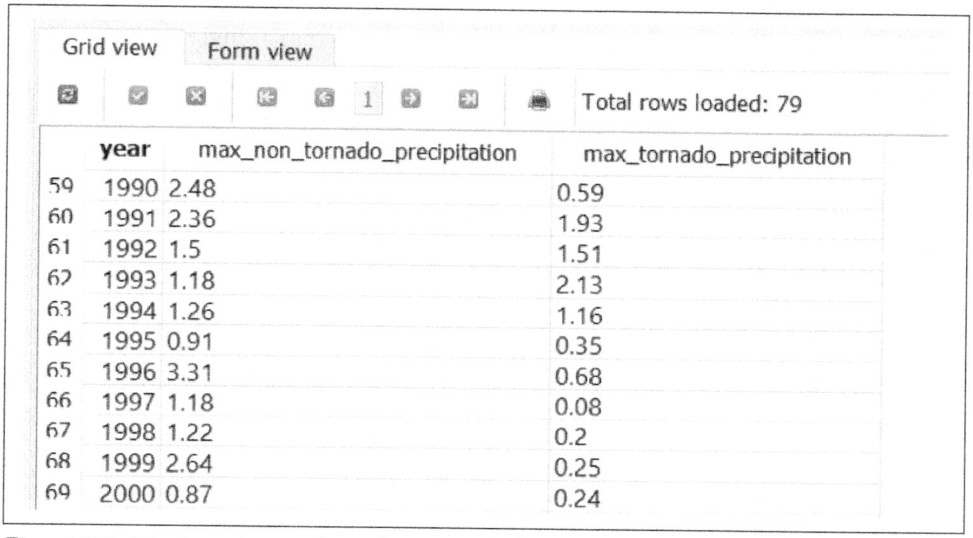

	year	max_non_tornado_precipitation	max_tornado_precipitation
59	1990	2.48	0.59
60	1991	2.36	1.93
61	1992	1.5	1.51
62	1993	1.18	2.13
63	1994	1.26	1.16
64	1995	0.91	0.35
65	1996	3.31	0.68
66	1997	1.18	0.08
67	1998	1.22	0.2
68	1999	2.64	0.25
69	2000	0.87	0.24

Figure 7-3. Maximum tornado and non-tornado precipitations by year

Just like with the WHERE statement, you can use any Boolean expressions in a CASE statement, including functions and AND, OR, and NOT statements. The following query will find the average temperatures by month when rain/hail was present versus not present after the year 2000:

```
SELECT month,

AVG(CASE WHEN rain OR hail THEN temperature ELSE null END)
AS avg_precipitation_temp,

AVG(CASE WHEN NOT (rain OR hail) THEN temperature ELSE null END)
AS avg_non_precipitation_temp

FROM STATION_DATA
WHERE year > 2000
GROUP BY month
```

The zero/null CASE trick is a great use of the CASE statement. It offers many possibilities to perform several aggregations with different criteria and therefore is worth knowing.

Summary

We dedicated a chapter to learning about CASE statements because they offer a lot of flexibility. We can swap values in a column with another set of values based on conditions we provide. When we aggregate CASE statements, we bring more possibilities to slice data in interesting ways and pack more information into a single query.

Hopefully by now you have a solid foundation and are ready to learn the defining part of SQL: the JOIN. Take a break. Down a few espressos. After you learn the JOIN, you can truly call yourself a SQL developer.

CHAPTER 8

JOIN

Stitching Tables Together

Joining is the defining functionality of SQL and sets it apart from other data technologies. Be sure you are somewhat comfortable with the material we've covered so far, and take your time practicing and reviewing before moving on.

Let's rewind back to the beginning of this book, when we were discussing relational databases. Remember how "normalized" databases often have tables with fields that point to other tables? For example, consider this CUSTOMER_ORDER table, which has a CUSTOMER_ID field (Figure 8-1).

	ORDER_ID	ORDER_DATE	SHIP_DATE	CUSTOMER_ID	PRODUCT_ID	ORDER_QTY	SHIPPED
1	3	2015-04-20	2015-04-23	3	5	300	false
2	4	2015-04-18	2015-04-22	5	4	375	false
3	1	2015-04-15	2015-04-18	1	1	450	false
4	5	2015-04-17	2015-04-20	3	2	500	false
5	2	2015-04-18	2015-04-21	3	2	600	false

Figure 8-1. The CUSTOMER_ORDER table has a CUSTOMER_ID field

This CUSTOMER_ID field gives us a *key* to look up in the table CUSTOMER. Knowing this, it should be no surprise that the CUSTOMER table also has a CUSTOMER_ID field (Figure 8-2).

CUSTOMER ID	NAME	REGION	STREET ADDRESS	CITY	STATE	ZIP
1	LITE Industrial	Southwest	729 Ravine Way	Irving	TX	75014
2	Rex Tooling Inc	Southwest	6129 Collie Blvd	Dallas	TX	75201
3	Re-Barre Construction	Southwest	9043 Windy Dr	Irving	TX	75032
4	Prairie Construction	Southwest	264 Long Rd	Moore	OK	62104
5	Marsh Lane Metal Works	Southeast	9143 Marsh Ln	Avondale	LA	79782

Figure 8-2. The CUSTOMER table has a CUSTOMER_ID key field that can be used to get customer information

We can retrieve customer information for an order from this table, very much like a VLOOKUP in Excel.

This is an example of a *relationship* between the CUSTOMER_ORDER table and the CUSTOMER table. We can say that CUSTOMER is a *parent* to CUSTOMER_ORDER. Because CUSTOMER_ORDER depends on CUSTOMER for information, it is a *child* of CUSTOMER. Conversely, CUSTOMER cannot be a child of CUSTOMER_ORDER because it does not rely on it for any information. The diagram in Figure 8-3 shows this relationship; the arrow shows that CUSTOMER supplies customer information to CUSTOMER_ORDER via the CUSTOMER_ID.

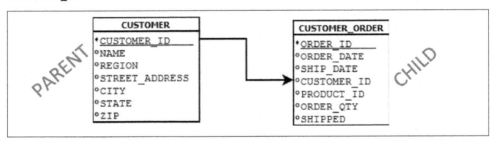

Figure 8-3. CUSTOMER is the parent to CUSTOMER_ORDER, because CUSTOMER_ORDER depends on it for CUSTOMER information

The other aspect to consider in a relationship is how many records in the child can be tied to a single record of the parent. Take the CUSTOMER and CUSTOMER_ORDER tables and you will see it is a *one-to-many relationship*, where a single customer record can line up with multiple orders. Let's take a look at Figure 8-4 to see a specific example: the customer "Re-Barre Construction" with CUSTOMER_ID 3 is tied to three orders.

CUSTOMER

CUSTOMER ID	NAME	REGION	STREET ADDRESS	CITY	STATE	ZIP
1	LITE Industrial	Southwest	729 Ravine Way	Irving	TX	75014
2	Rex Tooling Inc	Southwest	6129 Collie Blvd	Dallas	TX	75201
3	Re-Barre Construction	Southwest	9043 Windy Dr	Irving	TX	75032
4	Prairie Construction	Southwest	264 Long Rd	Moore	OK	62104
5	Marsh Lane Metal Works	Southeast	9143 Marsh Ln	Avondale	LA	79782

CUSTOMER_ORDER

	ORDER_ID	ORDER_DATE	SHIP_DATE	CUSTOMER_ID	PRODUCT_ID	ORDER_QTY	SHIPPED
1	3	2015-04-20	2015-04-23	3	5	300	false
2	4	2015-04-18	2015-04-22	5	4	375	false
3	1	2015-04-15	2015-04-18	1	1	450	false
4	5	2015-04-17	2015-04-20	3	2	500	false
5	2	2015-04-18	2015-04-21	3	2	600	false

Figure 8-4. A one-to-many relationship between CUSTOMER and CUSTOMER_ORDER

One-to-many is the most common type of relationship because it accommodates most business needs, such as a single customer having multiple orders. Business data in a well-designed database should strive for a one-to-many pattern. Less common are the *one-to-one* and *many-to-many relationships* (sometimes referred to as a Cartesian product). These are worth researching later, but in the interest of focusing the scope of this book, we will steer clear of them.

INNER JOIN

Understanding table relationships, we can consider that it might be nice to stitch two tables together, so we can see CUSTOMER and CUSTOMER_ORDER information alongside each other. Otherwise, we will have to manually perform tons of lookups with CUSTOMER_ID, which can be quite tedious. We can avoid that with JOIN operators, and we will start by learning the INNER JOIN.

The INNER JOIN allows us to merge two tables together. But if we are going to merge tables, we need to define a commonality between the two so records from both tables line up. We need to define one or more fields they have in common and join on them. If we are going to query the CUSTOMER_ORDER table and join it to CUSTOMER to bring in customer information, we need to define the commonality on CUSTOMER_ID.

Open up the rexon_metals database and open a new SQL editor window. We are going to execute our first INNER JOIN:

```
SELECT ORDER_ID,
CUSTOMER.CUSTOMER_ID,
ORDER_DATE,
SHIP_DATE,
NAME,
STREET_ADDRESS,
CITY,
STATE,
ZIP,
PRODUCT_ID,
ORDER_QTY

FROM CUSTOMER INNER JOIN CUSTOMER_ORDER
ON CUSTOMER.CUSTOMER_ID = CUSTOMER_ORDER.CUSTOMER_ID
```

The first thing you may notice is we were able to query fields from both CUSTOMER and CUSTOMER_ORDER. It is almost like we took those two tables and temporarily merged them into a single table, which we queried off of. In effect, that is exactly what we did!

Let's break down how this was accomplished. First, we select the fields we want from the CUSTOMER and CUSTOMER_ORDER tables:

```
SELECT CUSTOMER.CUSTOMER_ID,
NAME,
STREET_ADDRESS,
CITY,
STATE,
ZIP,
ORDER_DATE,
SHIP_DATE,
ORDER_ID,
PRODUCT_ID,
ORDER_QTY

FROM CUSTOMER INNER JOIN CUSTOMER_ORDER
ON CUSTOMER.CUSTOMER_ID = CUSTOMER_ORDER.CUSTOMER_ID
```

In this case, we want to show customer address information for each order. Also notice that because CUSTOMER_ID is in both tables, we had to explicitly choose one (although it should not matter which). In this case, we chose the CUSTOMER_ID in CUSTOMER using an explicit syntax, CUSTOMER.CUSTOMER_ID.

Finally, the important part that temporarily merges two tables into one. The FROM statement is where we execute our INNER JOIN. We specify that we are pulling from CUSTOMER and inner joining it with CUSTOMER_ORDER, and that the commonality is on the CUSTOMER_ID fields (which have to be equal to line up):

```
SELECT CUSTOMER.CUSTOMER_ID,
NAME,
STREET_ADDRESS,
CITY,
STATE,
ZIP,
ORDER_DATE,
SHIP_DATE,
ORDER_ID,
PRODUCT_ID,
ORDER_QTY

FROM CUSTOMER INNER JOIN CUSTOMER_ORDER
ON CUSTOMER.CUSTOMER_ID = CUSTOMER_ORDER.CUSTOMER_ID
```

If you have worked with Excel, think of this as a VLOOKUP on steroids, where instead of looking up CUSTOMER_ID and getting one value from another table, we are getting the entire matching record. This enables us to select any number of fields from the other table.

Now take a look at the results (Figure 8-5). Thanks to the INNER JOIN, this query gives us a view that includes the customer details with each order.

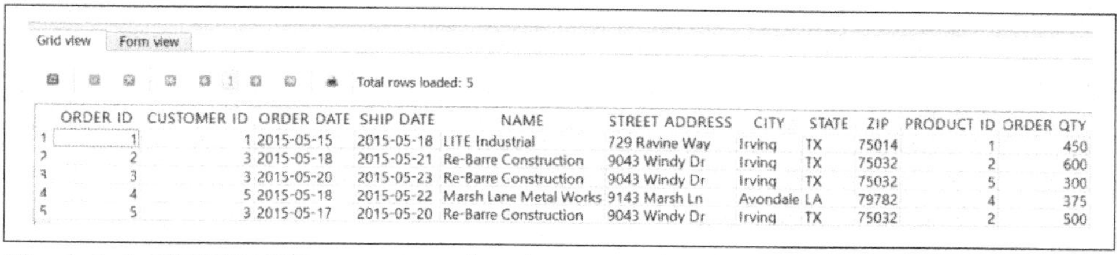

Figure 8-5. CUSTOMER inner joined with CUSTOMER_ORDER

Joins truly give us the best of both worlds. We store data efficiently through normalization, but can use joins to merge tables together on common fields to create more descriptive views of the data.

There is one behavior with INNER JOIN to be aware of. Take a moment to look at the results of the preceding query. We can see that we have three "Re-Barre Construction" orders, as well as an order from "LITE Industrial" and another from "Marsh Lane Metal Works." But are we missing anybody?

If you go look at the CUSTOMER table, you will see there are five customers. Our INNER JOIN query captured only three. "Rex Tooling Inc" and "Prairie Construction" are nowhere to be found in our query results. So what exactly happened? There are no orders for Rex Tooling Inc and Prairie Construction, and because of this the INNER JOIN excluded them from the query. It will only show records that inclusively exist in both tables (Figure 8-6).

CUSTOMER

CUSTOMER ID	NAME	REGION	STREET ADDRESS	CITY	STATE	ZIP
1	LITE Industrial	Southwest	729 Ravine Way	Irving	TX	75014
2	Rex Tooling Inc	Southwest	6129 Collie Blvd	Dallas	TX	75201
3	Re-Barre Construction	Southwest	9043 Windy Dr	Irving	TX	75032
4	Prairie Construction	Southwest	264 Long Rd	Moore	OK	62104
5	Marsh Lane Metal Works	Southeast	9143 Marsh Ln	Avondale	LA	79782

CUSTOMER_ORDER

ORDER ID	ORDER DATE	SHIP DATE	CUSTOMER ID	PRODUCT ID	ORDER QTY	SHIPPED
1	2015-05-15	2015-05-18	1	1	450	false
2	2015-05-18	2015-05-21	3	2	600	false
3	2015-05-20	2015-05-23	3	5	300	false
4	2015-05-18	2015-05-22	5	4	375	false
5	2015-05-17	2015-05-20	3	2	500	false

INNER JOINED

ORDER ID	CUSTOMER ID	ORDER DATE	SHIP DATE	NAME	STREET ADDRESS	CITY	STATE	ZIP	PRODUCT ID	ORDER QTY
1	1	2015-05-15	2015-05-18	LITE Industrial	729 Ravine Way	Irving	TX	75014	1	450
2	3	2015-05-18	2015-05-21	Re-Barre Construction	9043 Windy Dr	Irving	TX	75032	2	600
3	3	2015-05-20	2015-05-23	Re-Barre Construction	9043 Windy Dr	Irving	TX	75032	5	300
4	5	2015-05-18	2015-05-22	Marsh Lane Metal Works	9143 Marsh Ln	Avondale	LA	79782	4	375
5	3	2015-05-17	2015-05-20	Re-Barre Construction	9043 Windy Dr	Irving	TX	75032	2	500

Figure 8-6. A visualized inner join between CUSTOMER and CUSTOMER_ORDER (note the two customers getting omitted, as they have no orders to join to)

With an INNER JOIN, any records that do not have a common joined value in both tables will be excluded. If we want to include all records from the CUSTOMER table, we can accomplish this with a LEFT JOIN.

LEFT JOIN

Those two customers, Rex Tooling Inc and Prairie Construction, were excluded from the INNER JOIN on CUSTOMER_ID because they had no orders to join on. But suppose we did want to include them anyway. Often, we may want to join tables and see, for example, all customers, even if they had no orders.

If you are comfortable with the INNER JOIN, the left outer join is not much different. But there is one very subtle difference. Modify your query from before and replace the INNER JOIN with LEFT JOIN, the keywords for a left outer join. As shown in Figure 8-7, the table specified on the "left" side of the LEFT JOIN operator (CUSTOMER) will have all its records included, even if they do not have any child records in the "right" table (CUSTOMER_ORDER).

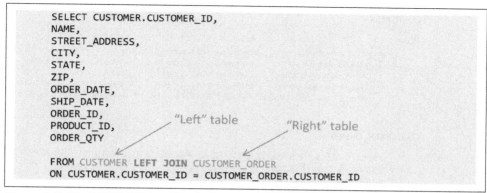

```
SELECT CUSTOMER.CUSTOMER_ID,
NAME,
STREET_ADDRESS,
CITY,
STATE,
ZIP,
ORDER_DATE,
SHIP_DATE,
ORDER_ID,
PRODUCT_ID,                "Left" table          "Right" table
ORDER_QTY


FROM CUSTOMER LEFT JOIN CUSTOMER_ORDER
ON CUSTOMER.CUSTOMER_ID = CUSTOMER_ORDER.CUSTOMER_ID
```

Figure 8-7. The LEFT JOIN will include all records on the "left" table, even if they have nothing to join to on the "right" table (which will be null)

Running this, we have similar results to what we got from the INNER JOIN query earlier, but we have two additional records for the customers that have no orders (Figure 8-8). For those two customers, notice all the fields that come from CUS TOMER_ORDER are null, because there were no orders to join to. Instead of omitting them like the INNER JOIN did, the LEFT JOIN just made them null (Figure 8-9).

CUSTOMER ID	NAME	STREET ADDRESS	CITY	STATE	ZIP	ORDER DATE	SHIP DATE	ORDER ID	PRODUCT ID	ORDER QTY
1	LITE Industrial	729 Ravine Way	Irving	TX	75014	2015-05-15	2015-05-18	1	1	450
2	Rex Tooling Inc	6129 Collie Blvd	Dallas	TX	75201	NULL	NULL	NULL	NULL	NULL
3	Re-Barre Construction	9043 Windy Dr	Irving	TX	75032	2015-05-17	2015-05-20	5	2	500
3	Re-Barre Construction	9043 Windy Dr	Irving	TX	75032	2015-05-18	2015-05-21	2	2	600
3	Re-Barre Construction	9043 Windy Dr	Irving	TX	75032	2015-05-20	2015-05-23	3	5	300
4	Prairie Construction	264 Long Rd	Moore	OK	62104	NULL	NULL	NULL	NULL	NULL
5	Marsh Lane Metal Works	9143 Marsh Ln	Avondale	LA	79782	2015-05-18	2015-05-22	4	4	375

Figure 8-8. CUSTOMER left joined with CUSTOMER_ORDER (note the null CUSTOMER_ORDER fields mean no orders were found for those two customers)

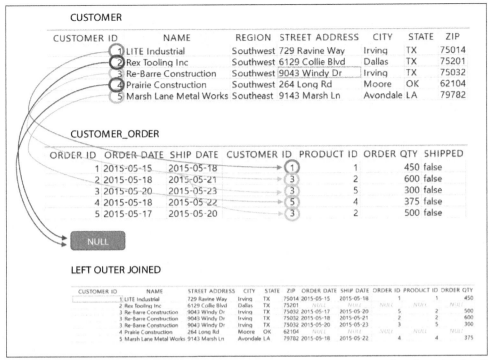

Figure 8-9. CUSTOMER left joined with CUSTOMER_ORDER (note that "Rex Tooling" and "Prairie Construction" joined to NULL, as they have no orders to join to)

It is also common to use LEFT JOIN to check for "orphaned" child records that have no parent, or conversely a parent that has no children (e.g., orders that have no customers, or customers that have no orders). You can use a WHERE statement to check for null values that are a result of the LEFT JOIN. Modifying our previous example, we can filter for customers that have no orders by filtering any field from the right table that is null:

```
SELECT
CUSTOMER.CUSTOMER_ID,
NAME AS CUSTOMER_NAME

FROM CUSTOMER LEFT JOIN CUSTOMER_ORDER
ON CUSTOMER.CUSTOMER_ID = CUSTOMER_ORDER.CUSTOMER_ID

WHERE ORDER_ID IS NULL
```

Sure enough, you will only see Rex Tooling Inc and Prairie Construction listed, as they have no orders.

Other JOIN Types

There is a RIGHT JOIN operator, which performs a right outer join that is almost identical to the left outer join. It flips the direction of the join and includes all records from the right table. However, the RIGHT JOIN is rarely used and should be avoided. You should stick to convention and prefer left outer joins with LEFT JOIN, and put the "all records" table on the left side of the join operator.

There also is a full outer join operator called OUTER JOIN that includes all records from both tables. It does a LEFT JOIN and a RIGHT JOIN simultaneously, and can have null records in both tables. It can be helpful to find orphaned records in both directions simultaneously in a single query, but it also is seldom used.

 RIGHT JOIN and OUTER JOIN are not supported in SQLite due to their highly niche nature. But most database solutions feature them.

Joining Multiple Tables

Relational databases can be fairly complex in terms of relationships between tables. A given table can be the child of more than one parent table, and a table can be the parent to one table but a child to another. So how does this all work?

We have observed the relationship between CUSTOMER and CUSTOMER_ORDER. But there is another table we can include that will make our orders more meaningful: the PRODUCT table. Notice that the CUSTOMER_ORDER table has a PRODUCT_ID column, which corresponds to a product in the PRODUCT table.

We can supply not only CUSTOMER information to the CUSTOMER_ORDER table, but also PRODUCT information using PRODUCT_ID (Figure 8-10).

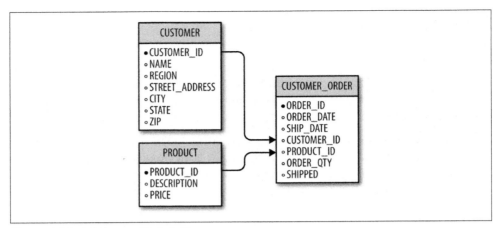

Figure 8-10. Joining multiple tables

We can use these two relationships to execute a query that displays orders with customer information and product information simultaneously. All we do is define the two joins between CUSTOMER_ORDER and CUSTOMER, and CUSTOMER_ORDER and PRODUCT (Figure 8-11). If you start to get confused, just compare the following query to the diagram in Figure 8-10, and you will see the joins are constructed strictly on these relationships:

```
SELECT
ORDER_ID,
CUSTOMER.CUSTOMER_ID,
NAME AS CUSTOMER_NAME,
STREET_ADDRESS,
CITY,
STATE,
ZIP,
ORDER_DATE,
PRODUCT_ID,
DESCRIPTION,
ORDER_QTY

FROM CUSTOMER

INNER JOIN CUSTOMER_ORDER
ON CUSTOMER_ORDER.CUSTOMER_ID = CUSTOMER.CUSTOMER_ID

INNER JOIN PRODUCT
ON CUSTOMER_ORDER.PRODUCT_ID = PRODUCT.PRODUCT_ID
```

ORDER ID	CUSTOMER ID	CUSTOMER NAME	STREET ADDRESS	CITY	STATE	ZIP	ORDER DATE	PRODUCT ID	DESCRIPTION	ORDER QTY
1	1	1 LITE Industrial	729 Ravine Way	Irving	TX	75014	2015-05-15	1	Copper	450
2	2	3 Re-Barre Construction	9043 Windy Dr	Irving	TX	75032	2015-05-18	2	Aluminum	600
3	3	3 Re-Barre Construction	9043 Windy Dr	Irving	TX	75032	2015-05-20	5	Bronze	300
4	4	5 Marsh Lane Metal Works	9143 Marsh Ln	Avondale	LA	79782	2015-05-18	4	Steel	375
5	5	3 Re-Barre Construction	9043 Windy Dr	Irving	TX	75032	2015-05-17	2	Aluminum	500

Figure 8-11. Joining ORDER, CUSTOMER, and PRODUCT fields together

These orders are much more descriptive now that we've leveraged `CUSTOMER_ID` and `PRODUCT_ID` to bring in customer and product information. As a matter of fact, now that we've merged these three tables, we can use fields from all three tables to create expressions. If we want to find the revenue for each order, we can multiply `ORDER_QTY` and `PRICE`, even though those fields exist in two separate tables:

```
SELECT
ORDER_ID,
CUSTOMER.CUSTOMER_ID,
NAME AS CUSTOMER_NAME,
STREET_ADDRESS,
CITY,
STATE,
ZIP,
ORDER_DATE,
PRODUCT_ID,
DESCRIPTION,
ORDER_QTY,
ORDER_QTY * PRICE as REVENUE

FROM CUSTOMER

INNER JOIN CUSTOMER_ORDER
ON CUSTOMER.CUSTOMER_ID = CUSTOMER_ORDER.CUSTOMER_ID

INNER JOIN PRODUCT
ON CUSTOMER_ORDER.PRODUCT_ID = PRODUCT.PRODUCT_ID
```

Now we have the revenue for each order, even though the needed columns came from two separate tables.

Grouping JOINs

Let's keep going with this example. We have the orders with their revenue, thanks to the join we built. But suppose we want to find the total revenue by customer? We still need to use all three tables and merge them together with our current join setup, because we need the revenue we just calculated. But also we need to do a `GROUP BY`.

This is legitimate and perfectly doable. Because we want to aggregate by customer, we need to group on `CUSTOMER_ID` and `CUSTOMER_NAME`. Then we need to `SUM` the

ORDER_QTY * PRICE expression to get total revenue (Figure 8-12). To focus our GROUP BY scope, we omit all other fields:

```
SELECT
CUSTOMER.CUSTOMER_ID,
NAME AS CUSTOMER_NAME,
sum(ORDER_QTY * PRICE) as TOTAL_REVENUE

FROM CUSTOMER_ORDER

INNER JOIN CUSTOMER
ON CUSTOMER.CUSTOMER_ID = CUSTOMER_ORDER.CUSTOMER_ID

INNER JOIN PRODUCT
ON CUSTOMER_ORDER.PRODUCT_ID = PRODUCT.PRODUCT_ID

GROUP BY 1,2
```

CUSTOMER ID	CUSTOMER NAME	TOTAL REVENUE
1	LITE Industrial	3379.5
3	Re-Barre Construction	4038.0
5	Marsh Lane Metal Works	4616.25

Figure 8-12. Calculating TOTAL_REVENUE by joining and aggregating three tables

Because we may want to see all customers, including ones that have no orders, we can use LEFT JOIN instead of INNER JOIN for all our join operations (Figure 8-13):

```
SELECT
CUSTOMER.CUSTOMER_ID,
NAME AS CUSTOMER_NAME,
sum(ORDER_QTY * PRICE) as TOTAL_REVENUE

FROM CUSTOMER

LEFT JOIN CUSTOMER_ORDER
ON CUSTOMER.CUSTOMER_ID = CUSTOMER_ORDER.CUSTOMER_ID

LEFT JOIN PRODUCT
ON CUSTOMER_ORDER.PRODUCT_ID = PRODUCT.PRODUCT_ID

GROUP BY 1,2
```

CUSTOMER ID	CUSTOMER NAME	TOTAL REVENUE
1	LITE Industrial	3379.5
2	Rex Tooling Inc	*NULL*
3	Re-Barre Construction	4038.0
4	Prairie Construction	*NULL*
5	Marsh Lane Metal Works	4616.25

Figure 8-13. Using a LEFT JOIN to include all customers and their TOTAL_REVENUE

We have to LEFT JOIN both table pairs, because mixing LEFT JOIN and INNER JOIN would cause the INNER JOIN to win, resulting in the two customers without orders getting excluded. This is because null values cannot be inner joined on and will always get filtered out. A LEFT JOIN tolerates null values.

Rex Tooling Inc and Prairie Construction are now present even though they have no orders. But we may want the values to default to 0 instead of null if there are no sales. We can accomplish this simply with the coalesce() function we learned about in Chapter 5 to turn nulls into zeros (Figure 8-14):

```
SELECT
CUSTOMER.CUSTOMER_ID,
NAME AS CUSTOMER_NAME,
coalesce(sum(ORDER_QTY * PRICE), 0) as TOTAL_REVENUE

FROM CUSTOMER

LEFT JOIN CUSTOMER_ORDER
ON CUSTOMER.CUSTOMER_ID = CUSTOMER_ORDER.CUSTOMER_ID

LEFT JOIN PRODUCT
ON CUSTOMER_ORDER.PRODUCT_ID = PRODUCT.PRODUCT_ID

GROUP BY 1,2
```

CUSTOMER_ID	CUSTOMER_NAME	TOTAL_REVENUE
1	LITE Industrial	3379.5
2	Rex Tooling Inc	0
3	Re-Barre Construction	4038.0
4	Prairie Construction	0
5	Marsh Lane Metal Works	4616.25

Figure 8-14. Coalescing null TOTAL_REVENUE values to 0

Summary

Joins are the most challenging topic in SQL, but they are also the most rewarding. Joins allow us to take data scattered across multiple tables and stitch it together into something more meaningful and descriptive. We can take two or more tables and join them together into a larger table that has more context. In the next chapter, we will learn more about joins and how they are naturally defined by table relationships.

CHAPTER 9

Database Design

Planning a Database

So far in this book, we have only learned how to be consumers of data with the SELECT statement. We have done analysis operations that read data and transform it in interesting ways, but none of this physically changes the data in the tables. A SELECT statement is a read-only operation. Sometimes, though, we will want to CREATE new tables, as well as INSERT, UPDATE, and DELETE records.

When you create your own tables to support your business, it should not be done lightly. You need to plan carefully because bad database design is sure to cause regrets down the road. There are critical questions that should drive your design:

Design questions
- What are the business requirements?
- What tables will I need to fulfill those requirements?
- What columns will each table contain?
- How will the tables be normalized?
- What will their parent/child relationships be?

It might be a good idea to draft a diagram showing the tables and how they are related. But design is not the only factor to consider. Populating data should be part of the planning process too. If the data is not maintainable and kept up to date, then the design has already failed. This factor is often overlooked and can easily cause a database project to fail.

Data questions
- How much data will be populated into these tables?
- Who/what will populate the data into these tables?
- Where will the data come from?
- Do we need processes to automatically populate the tables?

Data inception has to happen somewhere. Depending on the nature of the data, it can be created within your organization or received from an external party. If you need to store a high volume of data that updates regularly, chances are a human cannot do this task manually. You will need a process written in Java, Python, or another coding language to do that.

Although security and administration are beyond the scope of this book, centralized databases usually are concerned with these areas. Administrating privileges and security is a full-time job in itself and often done by database administrators (DBAs). For centralized databases, security factors should be considered.

Security questions
- Who should have access to this database?
- Who should have access to which tables? Read-only access? Write access?
- Is this database critical to business operations?
- What backup plans do we have in the event of disaster/failure?
- Should changes to tables be logged?
- If the database is used for websites or web applications, is it secure?

Security is often a tough topic to address. Excessive security creates bureaucracy and obstructs nimbleness, but insufficient security will invite calamity. Like with any complex issue, a balance between the two extremes has to be found. But security should become a high priority when the database is used for a website. Connecting anything to the Web makes it more vulnerable to leaks and malicious attacks.

One of the most common malicious hacks is *SQL injection*. If a web developer has failed to implement security measures in a website, you can type a carefully crafted SELECT statement right inside a web browser, and get the query results displayed right back to you! 130 million credit card numbers were stolen this way in 2009.

SQLite has few security or administrative features, as these features would be overkill in a lightweight database. If your SQLite databases need to be secured, protect the database files the same way you would any other file. Either hide them, copy them to a backup, or distribute copies to your coworkers so they do not have access to the "master copy."

With all these considerations in mind, let's design our first database.

The SurgeTech Conference

You are a staff member for the SurgeTech conference, a gathering of tech startup companies seeking publicity and investors. The organizer has tasked you with creating a database to manage the attendees, companies, presentations, rooms, and presentation attendance. How should this database be designed?

First, review the different entities and start thinking about how they will be structured into tables. This may seem like a large number of business asks to capture, but any complex problem can be broken down into simple components.

ATTENDEE

The attendees are registered guests (including some VIPs) who are checking out the tech startups. Each attendee's ID, name, phone number, email, and VIP status will need to be tracked.

Taking all this information, we may design the ATTENDEE table with these columns:

COMPANY

The startup companies need to be tracked as well. The company ID, company name, company description, and primary contact (who should be listed as an attendee) for each must be tracked:

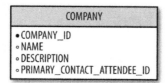

PRESENTATION

Some companies will schedule to do a presentation for a specific slot of time (with a start time and end time). The company leading the presentation as well as a room number must also be booked for each presentation slot:

ROOM

There will be rooms available for the presentations, each with a room ID number, a floor number, and a seating capacity:

PRESENTATION_ATTENDANCE

If attendees are interested in hearing a company's presentation, they can acquire a ticket (with a ticket ID) and be allowed in. This will help keep track of who attended what presentations. To implement this, the PRESENTATION_ATTENDANCE table will track the ticket IDs and pair the presentations with the attendees through their respective IDs to show who was where:

Primary and Foreign Keys

You should always strive to have a primary key on any table. A *primary key* is a special field (or combination of fields) that provides a unique identity to each record. A primary key often defines a relationship and is frequently joined on. The ATTENDEE table has an `ATTENDEE_ID` field as its primary key, `COMPANY` has `COMPANY_ID`, and so on. While you do not need to designate a field as a primary key to join on it, it allows the database software to execute queries much more efficiently. It also acts as a constraint to ensure data integrity. No duplicates are allowed on the primary key, which means you cannot have two `ATTENDEE` records both with an `ATTENDEE_ID` of 2. The database will forbid this from happening and throw an error.

 To focus our scope in this book, we will not compose a primary key off more than one field. But be aware that multiple fields can act as a primary key, and you can never have duplicate combinations of those fields. For example, if you specified your primary key on the fields `REPORT_ID` and `APPROVER_ID`, you can never have two records with the same combination of `REPORT_ID` and `APPROVER_ID`.

Do not confuse the primary key with a *foreign key*. The primary key exists in the parent table, but the foreign key exists in the child table. The foreign key in a child table points to the primary key in its parent table. For example, the `ATTENDEE_ID` in the `ATTENDEE` table is a primary key, but the `ATTENDEE_ID` in the `PRESENTATION_ATTENDANCE` table is a foreign key. The two are joined together for a one-to-many relationship. Unlike a primary key, a foreign key does not enforce uniqueness, as it is the "many" in a "one-to-many" relationship.

The primary key and foreign key do not have to share the same field name. The `BOOKED_COMPANY_ID` in the `PRESENTATION` table is a foreign key pointing to the `COMPANY_ID` in its parent table `COMPANY`. The field name can be different on the foreign key to make it more descriptive of its usage. In this case, `BOOKED_COMPANY_ID` is more descriptive than just `COMPANY_ID`. The semantics are subjective but still legitimate as long as the business wording is clear.

The Schema

Applying our knowledge of primary keys and foreign keys, we can establish the relationships between these five tables and draw a database schema as shown in Figure 9-1. A *database schema* is a diagram showing tables, their columns, and their relationships. All the primary keys and foreign keys are connected by arrows. The non-tipped side of the arrow ties to a primary key, while the tipped side points to a foreign key. These arrows visualize how each parent table supplies data to a child table.

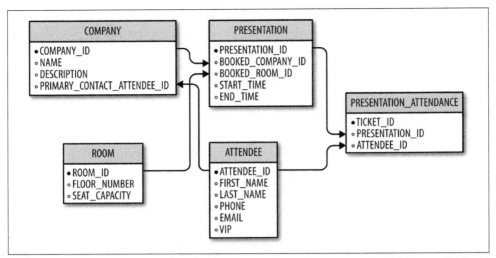

Figure 9-1. The database schema for the SurgeTech conference, with all tables and relationships

It can be overwhelming to look at these tables and relationships all at once. But all complex structures can be broken down into simple pieces. Chances are you will never write a SELECT query that uses all the tables, and you probably will only SELECT from two (maybe three) tables. Therefore, the secret to observing a schema is to focus only on two or three tables and their relationships at a time. While you analyze your drafted design, you can ensure the tables are efficiently normalized and primary/foreign keys are used effectively (Figure 9-2).

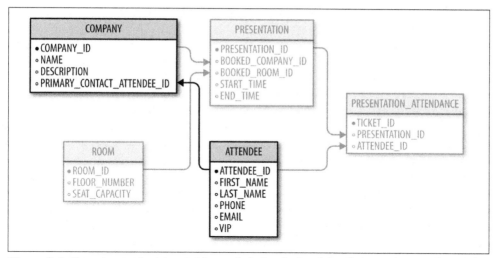

Figure 9-2. Focusing on just two tables and their relationships (here we can easily see the PRIMARY_CONTACT_ATTENDEE_ID supplies name and contact information from the ATTENDEE table)

If you can successfully visualize different SELECT queries and joins you would typically use on the data, the database schema is probably sound.

Creating a New Database

With a well-planned design, it is now time to actually create this database. We are going to use SQLiteStudio's tools to create the tables and components. But along the way, SQLiteStudio will show us the SQL it uses to create and modify our tables.

First, navigate to Database→Add a Database (Figure 9-3).

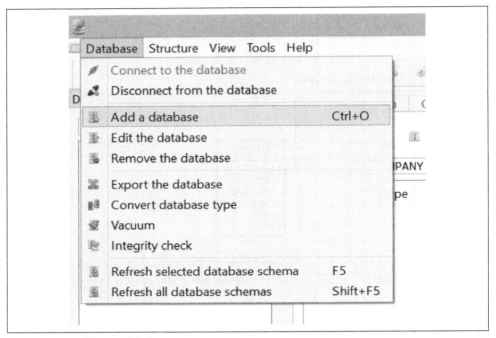

Figure 9-3. Adding a database

Click the green "plus" button circled in Figure 9-4 to create a new database.

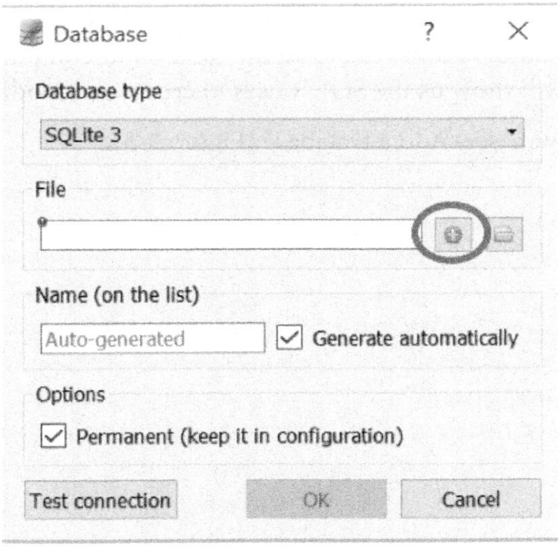

Figure 9-4. Creating a database

Browse to the folder you would like to save the database to. In the "File name" field, provide a name for the database file. It usually is good practice to end the name with the file extension *.db*. In this case, we might name it *surgetech_conference.db* (Figure 9-5).

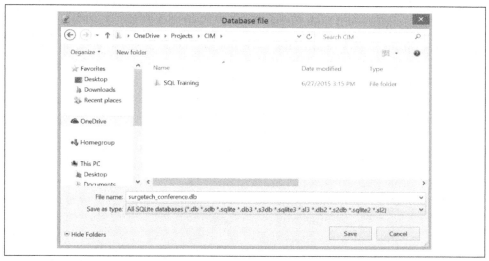

Figure 9-5. Selecting a location to create a database

Click Save, then OK. You should now see the new database in your navigator (Figure 9-6).

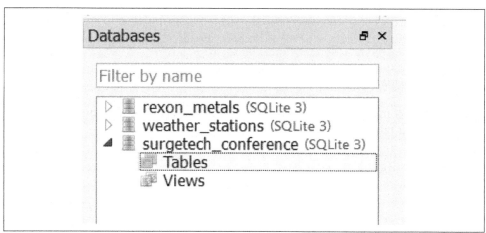

Figure 9-6. Our new surgetech_conference database

This database is empty, so next we will add some tables to it.

CREATE TABLE

When we create a table in SQL, we use a `CREATE TABLE` statement. However, I am an advocate for using tools that make tasks easier. We are going to use SQLiteStudio's visual tools to create the table, and when we are done it will generate and display the `CREATE TABLE` statement it built for us.

Right-click on the Tables item in the navigator and click Create a table, as shown in Figure 9-7.

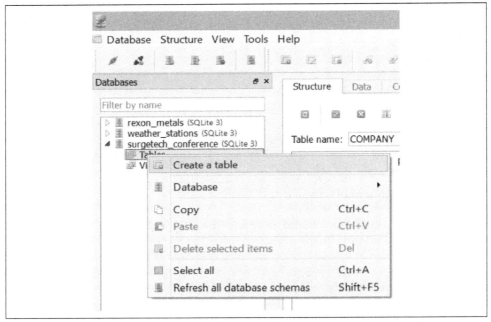

Figure 9-7. Creating a table

You will then come to the table Structure tab. Here we add, modify, and remove columns from our table (Figure 9-8).

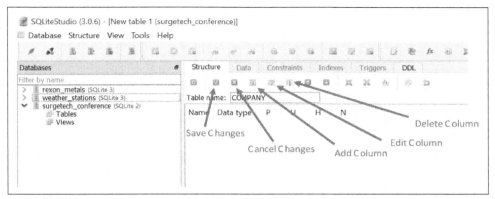

Figure 9-8. The table Structure tab, which we can use to add, modify, and remove columns from a table

We can also define various *constraints* to ensure data entered into the columns conforms to rules we specify. We also supply a name for this table in the "Table name" field. Type in **COMPANY** for this table name. Also note there is a button to save your edits and another to add a new column.

Click the Add Column button, and you will see a dialog to define a new column and its attributes. Name this column *COMPANY_ID* and make its data type "INTEGER," as shown in Figure 9-9.

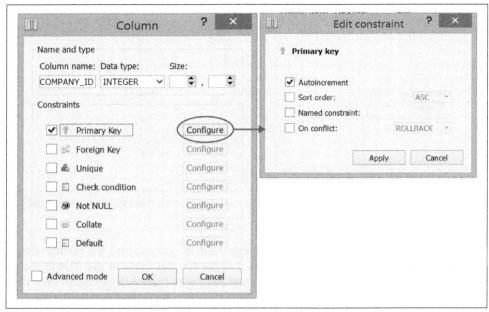

Figure 9-9. Defining a new COMPANY_ID column that holds integers; it also is configured to be the primary key and will automatically populate a value via "Autoincrement" for each inserted record

This is the COMPANY_ID field, and we need to define this as the primary key for the COMPANY table. Typically, the easiest way to assign key values is to do it sequentially for each new record. The first record will have a COMPANY_ID of 1, then the second record will have 2, then 3, and so on. When we INSERT records in the next chapter, this is a pain to do manually. But we can configure SQLite to automatically assign an ID for each record we insert. Simply check Primary Key, then click Configure, then select Autoincrement and click Apply (Figure 9-9).

Finally, click OK in the Column window and you will see our first column defined (Figure 9-10).

Figure 9-10. Our first column is defined; notice the key symbol indicating this column is the primary key

We have now defined our first column, and because it was the primary key column, it took some extra work. The rest of the columns will be a little easier to set up.

Click on the Add Column button again to create another column (Figure 9-11). Label this column *NAME* and make it a *VARCHAR* type, which is for text that can be of varying lengths. Specify the maximum number of characters to be 30. Because we likely never want this field to be null, check the "Not NULL" constraint. If any records are added or modified with NAME set to null, then the database will reject the edits.

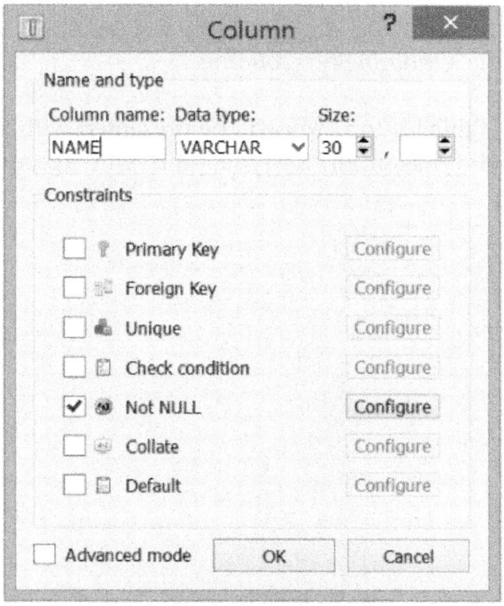

Figure 9-11. Creating a "NAME" column with type VARCHAR, a max character length of 30, and a "Not NULL" constraint

Click OK and then create two more columns, *DESCRIPTION* and *PRIMARY_CON-TACT_ATTENDEE_ID*, with the configurations shown in Figure 9-12. Note that *PRI-MARY_CONTACT_ATTENDEE_ID* should be a foreign key, but we have not defined that yet. We will come back to configure this after we have created its parent, the ATTENDEE table.

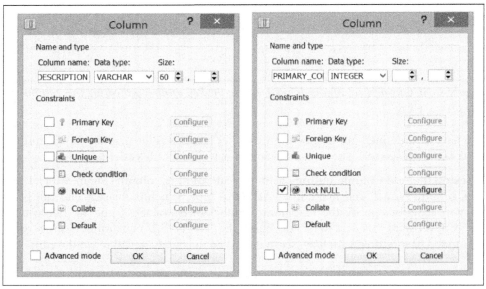

Figure 9-12. Creating the remaining two columns

Finally, click the Save Table button. You will be presented with a CREATE TABLE statement that SQLiteStudio has built for you, and will execute on your approval (Figure 9-13).

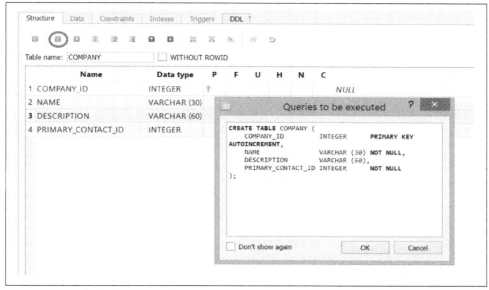

Figure 9-13. Click the Save Table button in the top toolbar, and SQLiteStudio will present the CREATE TABLE statement it is about to execute based on our inputted definitions

How cool is that? SQLiteStudio wrote SQL for you based on all the table definitions you built. Before you click OK, let's take a quick look at the CREATE TABLE statement to see how it works:

```
CREATE TABLE COMPANY (
    COMPANY_ID INTEGER PRIMARY KEY AUTOINCREMENT,
    NAME VARCHAR(30) NOT NULL,
    DESCRIPTION VARCHAR(60),
    PRIMARY_CONTACT_ID INTEGER NOT NULL
);
```

If you inspect the SQL query, you will see the CREATE TABLE statement declares a new table named COMPANY. After that, everything in parentheses defines the table columns. Each table column is defined by a name, followed by its type, and then any constraints or rules such as PRIMARY KEY, AUTOINCREMENT, or NOT NULL.

You could literally copy this statement and execute it in the SQL editor, but just click OK and it will execute the statement for you. After that, you should see your new table in the navigator (Figure 9-14).

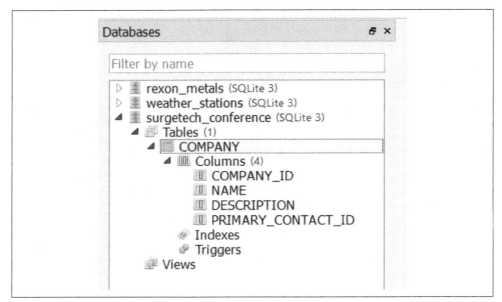

Figure 9-14. The COMPANY table in the navigator

The AUTOINCREMENT constraint in SQLite is actually not necessary. We use it here for practice because it is necessary for other platforms, including MySQL. In SQLite, making a column of type INTEGER a primary key will automatically make it handle its own ID assignment. As a matter of fact, it is actually more efficient in SQLite to not use AUTOINCREMENT and let the primary key implicitly do it.

Create the remaining four tables in the same manner. The needed CREATE TABLE statements are shown here (you can choose to build the tables using the Structure tab or just execute the CREATE TABLE statements verbatim in the SQL editor):

```
CREATE TABLE ROOM (
    ROOM_ID        INTEGER PRIMARY KEY AUTOINCREMENT,
    FLOOR_NUMBER   INTEGER NOT NULL,
    SEAT_CAPACITY  INTEGER NOT NULL
);

CREATE TABLE PRESENTATION (
    PRESENTATION_ID    INTEGER PRIMARY KEY AUTOINCREMENT,
    BOOKED_COMPANY_ID  INTEGER NOT NULL,
    BOOKED_ROOM_ID     INTEGER NOT NULL,
    START_TIME         TIME,
    END_TIME           TIME
);
```

```
CREATE TABLE ATTENDEE (
    ATTENDEE_ID INTEGER      PRIMARY KEY AUTOINCREMENT,
    FIRST_NAME  VARCHAR (30) NOT NULL,
    LAST_NAME   VARCHAR (30) NOT NULL,
    PHONE       INTEGER,
    EMAIL       VARCHAR (30),
    VIP         BOOLEAN      DEFAULT (0)
);

CREATE TABLE PRESENTATION_ATTENDANCE (
    TICKET_ID        INTEGER PRIMARY KEY AUTOINCREMENT,
    PRESENTATION_ID INTEGER,
    ATTENDEE_ID      INTEGER
);
```

Note that the ATTENDEE table has a VIP field which is a Boolean (true/false) value. By default, if a record does not specify a value for a column, the value will default to null. It might be a good idea to default this particular field to false (0) if a value is never provided. The preceding SQL snippet reflects this, but you can also accomplish this in the column builder as shown in Figure 9-15.

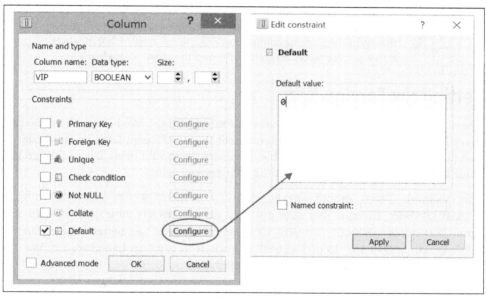

Figure 9-15. Setting a default value for a column

By now, you should have all five of your tables created with all constraints defined, except the foreign keys (Figure 9-16).

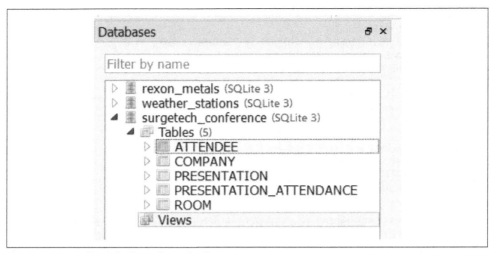

Figure 9-16. All tables have been built

Most database solutions enforce values in a column only by the specified data type. SQLite does not. In SQLite, you can put a TEXT value in an INTEGER column. Other database solutions will disallow this. While this seems counterintuitive, the creators of SQLite made it this way for technical reasons beyond the scope of this book.

Setting the Foreign Keys

There is one last task remaining to make our tables airtight. We have defined the primary keys but not the foreign keys. Remember that the foreign key in a child table is tied to the primary key of a parent table. Logically, we should never have a foreign key value that does not have a corresponding primary key value.

For example, we should never have a PRESENTATION record with a BOOKED_COMPANY_ID value that does not exist in the COMPANY table's COMPANY_ID column. If there is a BOOKED_COMPANY_ID value of 5, there had better be a record in COMPANY with a COMPANY_ID of 5 as well. Otherwise, it is an orphaned record. We can enforce this by setting up foreign key constraints.

Open up the PRESENTATION table and double-click the BOOKED_COMPANY_ID column to modify it (Figure 9-17). Check Foreign Key and then click Configure. Set the foreign table to CUSTOMER and the foreign column to CUSTOMER_ID. This will constrain BOOKED_COMPANY_ID to only the values in the CUSTOMER_ID column in the CUSTOMER table. Click Apply, then OK.

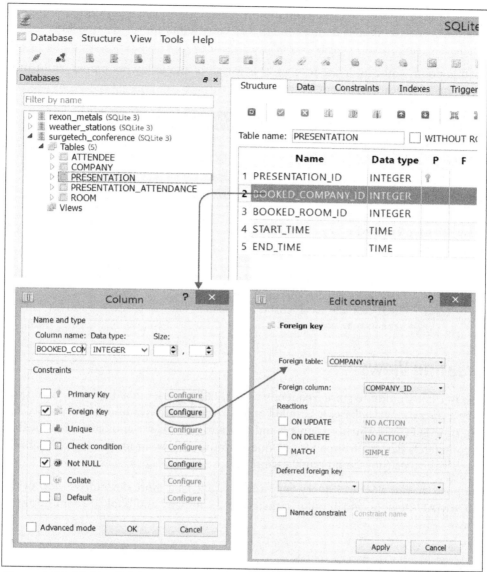

Figure 9-17. Making BOOKED_COMPANY_ID a foreign key to COMPANY_ID in the COMPANY table

Click the Commit Changes button on the Structure tab, and a series of SQL statements will be generated to implement the foreign key. You can look at the SQL if you are curious, but it will only make you appreciate all the work that SQLiteStudio has done for you. Then click OK to commit the change.

Using foreign keys keeps data tight and prevents deviant data from undermining the relationships. We should define foreign key constraints for all relationships in this database so no orphan records ever occur.

At this point, you can create foreign keys for all of the following parent–child relationships by repeating the same procedure:

Create foreign key for [Table].[Field]	Off parent primary key [Table].[Field]
PRESENTATION.BOOKED_ROOM_ID	ROOM.ROOM_ID
PRESENTATION_ATTENDANCE.PRESENTATION_ID	PRESENTATION.PRESENTATION_ID
PRESENTATION_ATTENDANCE.ATTENDEE_ID	ATTENDEE.ATTENDEE_ID
COMPANY.PRIMARY_CONTACT_ATTENDEE_ID	ATTENDEE.ATTENDEE_ID

Now we have ensured every child record has a parent record, and no orphans will ever be allowed into the database.

 If you ever use SQLite outside SQLiteStudio, note that the foreign key constraint enforcement might have to be turned on first. SQLiteStudio has it enabled by default, but other SQLite environments may not.

Creating Views

It is not uncommon to store frequently used SELECT queries in a database. When you save a query in a database, it is called a *view*. A view behaves much like a table. You can run SELECT statements against it and join it to other views and tables. But the data is completely derived from a SELECT query you specify, so in many cases you cannot modify the data (nor would it make sense to).

Suppose we run a SELECT query very often to give us a more descriptive view of the PRESENTATION table, which pulls in the booked company and booked room information:

```
SELECT
COMPANY.NAME as BOOKED_COMPANY,
ROOM.ROOM_ID as ROOM_NUMBER,
ROOM.FLOOR_NUMBER as FLOOR,
ROOM.SEAT_CAPACITY as SEATS,
START_TIME,
END_TIME

FROM PRESENTATION
```

```
INNER JOIN COMPANY
ON PRESENTATION.BOOKED_COMPANY_ID = COMPANY.COMPANY_ID

INNER JOIN ROOM
ON PRESENTATION.BOOKED_ROOM_ID = ROOM.ROOM_ID
```

Now suppose we want to store this query in the database so it can easily be called. We can do that by right-clicking the Views item in the navigator, then clicking Create a view (Figure 9-18).

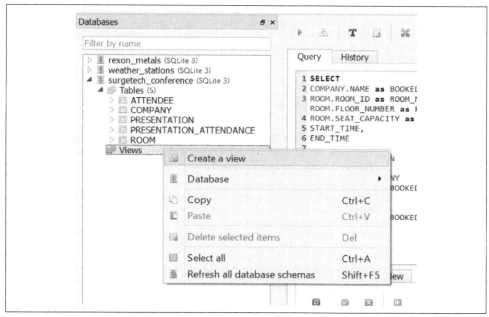

Figure 9-18. Creating a view

You will then be taken to a view designer window (Figure 9-19). Navigate to the Query tab. Here you will paste your SELECT statement. In the "View name" field, name this view ***PRESENTATION_VW*** (with "VW" an abbreviation for "VIEW"), and click the green checkmark to save it. Before it executes the SQL query to create the view, SQLiteStudio will present it for review. As you can observe, the SQL syntax to create a view is fairly simple. It is CREATE VIEW *[view_name]* AS *[a SELECT query]*.

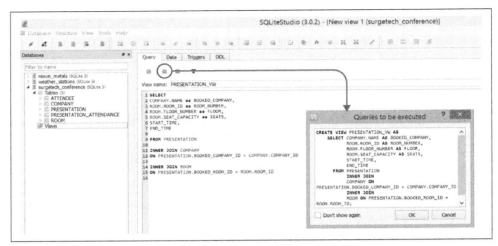

Figure 9-19. Creating a view off a SELECT query

When you click OK, you should now see the view in your navigator under "Views" (Figure 9-20). Double-click on it and in the Query tab you will see the query it is using, and the Data tab will have the query results.

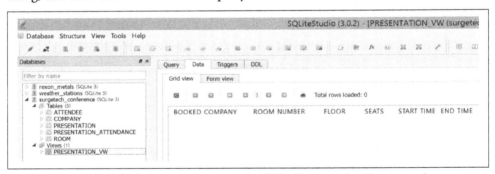

Figure 9-20. Although there is no data yet, the SELECT query has been saved as a view called PRESENTATION_VW

The Data tab will be blank, until the queried tables are populated with data.

Note also that we can query from a view just like it was a table (and apply filters, do join operations, and do anything else you could do in a SELECT with a table):

```
SELECT * FROM PRESENTATION_VW
WHERE SEAT_CAPACITY >= 30
```

Summary

In this chapter, we dived into creating our own databases and learned how to design them efficiently. We studied table relationships, which help us clearly define how tables are joined. We also explored some of the various column constraints (including PRIMARY KEY, FOREIGN KEY, NOT NULL, AUTOINCREMENT, and DEFAULT) to keep data consistent and ensure it follows rules we define.

In the next chapter, we will actually populate and modify data in this database. We will witness our design at work and appreciate the time we put into planning it. A good design with well-defined constraints will make a resilient database.

One topic this chapter did not cover is indexes. Indexes are useful for tables with a large number of records but have performance issues with SELECT statements. "APPENDIX B2 – Improving Performance with Indexes" on page 108 discusses indexes and when and when not to use them.

CHAPTER 10

Managing Data

In the previous chapter, we learned not only how to create a database but how to do it well. Well-considered table design, column constraints, and relationships will really shine once we start putting data into the tables. With our strong table design and the well-thought-out relationships between them, we will be able to join efficiently and easily. When a piece of data needs to be changed (e.g., a customer address), we only need to change it in one place rather than several. When a bad piece of data comes in, hopefully we have set enough sensible constraints to prevent it from entering the database.

In this chapter, we will learn how to INSERT, DELETE, and UPDATE records. Fortunately, writing operations like these is much simpler than writing SELECT statements.

These SQL write operations do not have to be done by a human. Software (written in Java, Python, or other coding languages) will often generate and execute SQL statements to read and write data the same way a human would, but much more efficiently. Although this is beyond the scope of this book, coding languages will be touched on in the next chapter if that is pertinent to you.

INSERT

In a relational database, data only exists if the database first receives records. The INSERT statement does just that and inserts a record into the database. You can pick what fields to populate in the record, and the rest of the fields will be null or use a default value.

First, we will INSERT an ATTENDEE record into the SurgeTech database we created in the last chapter. An INSERT to add yourself to the database should look something like this. Execute the following statement with your name:

```
INSERT INTO ATTENDEE (FIRST_NAME, LAST_NAME)
VALUES ('Thomas','Nield')
```

Let's break this statement down:

```
INSERT INTO ATTENDEE (FIRST_NAME, LAST_NAME)
VALUES ('Thomas','Nield')
```

To start, we declare that we are inserting a record into the ATTENDEE table, and the fields we are choosing to populate are FIRST_NAME and LAST_NAME:

```
INSERT INTO ATTENDEE (FIRST_NAME, LAST_NAME)
VALUES ('Thomas','Nield')
```

Then we specify the values for each of these fields. Note that we specify the values in the same order we declared the fields in: 'Thomas' corresponds to FIRST_NAME, and 'Nield' to LAST_NAME.

Run SELECT * FROM ATTENDEE to see if our INSERT made it in. Sure enough, the record now exists (Figure 10-1).

Figure 10-1. Our newly inserted record in the ATTENDEE table

There are a number of observations to make here. We did not populate all the columns in our INSERT, but due to the rules we created in the previous chapter, some of the columns were assigned a default value.

The ATTENDEE_ID gave itself a value of 1 due to our PRIMARY KEY and AUTOINCREMENT rule. If we were to INSERT another record, it would automatically be assigned an ATTENDEE_ID of 2, then 3, and so on. On an INSERT, you should avoid populating the ATTENDEE_ID field yourself and let it assign its own ID.

Again, the AUTOINCREMENT constraint in SQLite is actually not necessary. It is needed for MySQL and other platforms, though, hence why we are doing it for practice. In SQLite, simply making a column of type INTEGER a primary key will automatically assign IDs to new records.

PHONE and EMAIL were not specified in our INSERT, so they were left null. If either of these columns had a NOT NULL constraint and no default value policy, our INSERT would have failed. But in our design, we have allowed these two fields to be null in case our attendees prefer to be off the grid.

The VIP status was not specified in our INSERT either, but we gave this field a default value of false (0). So instead of making it null, SQLite resorted to using the default value we specified.

Hopefully by now, you are already appreciating that the design is working efficiently. Because of the policies we set, the columns resorted to default values when they were not provided with any.

Multiple INSERTs

If you have a lot of records to INSERT, you do not have to do it one at a time. You can specify multiple records in a single INSERT command. Simply repeat the clause following VALUES and separate each entry with a comma:

```
INSERT INTO ATTENDEE (FIRST_NAME, LAST_NAME, PHONE, EMAIL, VIP)
VALUES
('Jon', 'Skeeter',4802185842,'john.skeeter@rex.net', 1),
('Sam','Scala',2156783401,'sam.scala@gmail.com', 0),
('Brittany','Fisher',5932857296,'brittany.fisher@outlook.com', 0)
```

Doing multiple inserts in this manner is far more efficient, especially if you have thousands of records. If a process written in Java or Python is populating a table, it should use this syntax to insert large amounts of records rather than executing one INSERT at a time. Otherwise, the process can run very slowly.

You can also INSERT records using the results from a SELECT query. This is helpful if you need to migrate data from one table to another. Just make sure the SELECT fields line up with the INSERT fields and have the same order and data types:

```
INSERT INTO ATTENDEE (FIRST_NAME, LAST_NAME, PHONE, EMAIL)
SELECT FIRST_NAME, LAST_NAME, PHONE, EMAIL
FROM SOME_OTHER_TABLE
```

Testing the Foreign Keys

Let's take an opportunity to witness another policy of our design at work: the foreign keys.

Right now, we should only have four attendees with ATTENDEE_ID assignments of 1, 2, 3, and 4. But test this functionality by inserting a COMPANY record with a PRIMARY_CONTACT_ID value of 5:

```
INSERT INTO COMPANY (NAME, DESCRIPTION, PRIMARY_CONTACT_ID)
VALUES ('RexApp Solutions', 'A mobile app delivery service', 5)
```

This query should have failed and an error should be displayed at the bottom of the window (Figure 10-2).

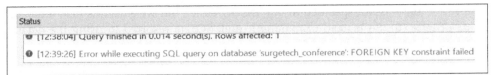

Figure 10-2. The foreign key constraint successfully raised an error

This is good because it means our foreign key constraint has worked: it kept an orphan record out. The INSERT needs to have a PRIMARY_CONTACT_ID that is existent. So, if we change it to 3 (Sam Scala), the INSERT should now work correctly:

```
INSERT INTO COMPANY (NAME, DESCRIPTION, PRIMARY_CONTACT_ID)
VALUES ('RexApp Solutions', 'A mobile app delivery service', 3)
```

DELETE

The DELETE statement is dangerously simple. It deletes all records in a table:

```
DELETE FROM ATTENDEE
```

However, you can conditionally delete records with a WHERE statement. If we wanted to remove all records that have no contact information, we could filter to records where PHONE and EMAIL are null:

```
DELETE FROM ATTENDEE
WHERE PHONE IS NULL
AND EMAIL IS NULL
```

Because it is perilously easy to make mistakes with a DELETE statement, it is a good practice to replace the DELETE with a SELECT * first. Executing that query gives us a preview of what records will be deleted:

```
SELECT * FROM ATTENDEE
WHERE PHONE IS NULL
AND EMAIL IS NULL
```

TRUNCATE TABLE

In the previous section, we looked at a means to delete all records from a table:

```
DELETE FROM ATTENDEE
```

Although not used in SQLite, on some database platforms (like MySQL) the preferred way to delete all records from a table is to use TRUNCATE TABLE:

```
TRUNCATE TABLE ATTENDEE
```

Using this command will allow the database engine to reset the autoincrements for any primary keys as well as any other constraint behaviors. It also allows it to make some optimizations behind the scenes to reset the table.

While SQLite does not support TRUNCATE TABLE, it does allow some similar optimizations when you run a DELETE without a WHERE.

UPDATE

Finally, we come to the UPDATE command. The UPDATE modifies existing records. If we wanted to update the EMAIL values for all records to be uppercase, we could do that with this statement using the UPPER() function:

```
UPDATE ATTENDEE SET EMAIL = UPPER(EMAIL)
```

We can also update multiple fields at once. Just separate each expression after the SET keyword with a comma. To update both the FIRST_NAME and LAST_NAME fields to uppercase, run this command:

```
UPDATE ATTENDEE SET FIRST_NAME = UPPER(FIRST_NAME),
LAST_NAME = UPPER(LAST_NAME)
```

Like with DELETE, we can use a WHERE to conditionally apply updates to records. Execute the following query to set the VIP field to true where the ATTENDEE_ID is 3 or 4:

```
UPDATE ATTENDEE SET VIP = 1
WHERE ATTENDEE_ID IN (3,4)
```

DROP TABLE

There may be times where you want to remove a table altogether from the database. Just type DROP TABLE followed by the name of the table you want to delete (this is a dangerous statement as well because it deletes the table permanently, so be careful and certain about what you are doing):

```
DROP TABLE MY_UNWANTED_TABLE
```

Summary

At this point, you have the tools you need to go out and create your own database and manage its data. You may have questions on how to do all of this efficiently or provide practical means for users to input and update data, because chances are you cannot teach all of them SQL and they will want a graphical user interface. Or maybe you want to know how to pump large amounts of data into a database automatically or synchronize it with another data source. This will be lightly addressed in the final chapter.

CHAPTER 11

Going Forward

If you have gotten to this chapter and covered all the material to this point, congrats! You have learned an adaptable and marketable skillset that can be applied to the fields of business, information technology, and engineering. With consistent practice and usage, you should feel comfortable positioning yourself professionally with SQL and database design.

When it comes to understanding and using technology, everyone has a different level of ambition. You may very well have read this book and see this material as not central to your career goals, but rather complementary. This may be the case if you are an interdepartmental manager of sorts and just want to understand IT a little better. You may feel this book has given all the insight you need, which is perfectly acceptable. Only you can define your career goals and prioritize what maximizes your value!

But perhaps SQL has really clicked with you, and you have questions on how you can do more. Maybe you want to have a deeper knowledge of SQL and business intelligence. Or maybe you want to create software and graphical user interfaces that interact with a database. After reading this material, you may feel you are not done and have unanswered questions on how to create full business solutions. If this is you, I encourage you to keep researching and pursuing whatever knowledge you need to fulfill your goals.

If you want to learn more detailed functionalities in SQL, there are plenty of books and resources available. You can expand your SQL knowledge with more advanced functionalities like subqueries and triggers. If you want a deep understanding of SQLite, check out *Using SQLite* by Jay A. Kreibich (O'Reilly). You can also pursue learning another database platform like MySQL in greater detail. But whatever you do, do not hesitate to use the Internet as a resource. It has an infinite number of tutorials, guides, walkthroughs, and documentation to help you expand your knowledge.

While SQL alone can increase your opportunities, you can become very adaptable by learning another relevant technology or two. If you are eager to expand your skillsets, then consider learning and integrating another topic. This will open dozens of career paths. Integrating a few technology skillsets can make you even more marketable than just specializing in one skillset.

Python is a great programming language that is accessible to beginners, and yet is powerful enough to be used by professional programmers and security testing hackers alike. You can use Python to process data into databases or write applications and processes that support a business. It is an adaptable programming language and pairs well with database development. A great resource to get started with Python is Al Sweigart's popular book *Automate the Boring Stuff with Python* (No Starch Press).

R can be used for business intelligence programming. R is a statistics programming language used to perform deep machine learning and analysis on data. I have noticed it is preferred by the business/science/math crowd because it focuses on those areas very well. It has endless functionalities to analyze anything from DNA sequences to business market trends. It does a great job applying classic statistical models like linear regression. I have not used many resources on R, but I have heard Coursera (*https://www.coursera.org/*) offers some great online courses on it.

Python's adaptability is catching up with R, as it now features libraries for data mining. Both technologies are free and open source. When a SELECT statement does not provide enough functionality for a specific question you have about your data, Python and R are powerful tools to glean that information.

If you are interested in full-blown software development and not just casual scripting, languages such as Java, Apple's Swift, or Microsoft's C# are great to pick up. With these languages you can make commercial-grade business software solutions and mobile apps. Full-blown programming can take many hours to master, and it is challenging. But if you become good at it, the work and opportunities are endless. If you decide to pursue Java, Herbert Schildt's *Java: A Beginner's Guide* (McGraw Hill Professional) is a good book to start with.

These definitely are not the only career paths you can take. Technology needs are so niche nowadays, you may adapt yourself into a role that never has been done before. Just be sure to focus on learning material that is pertinent to your immediate needs. On top of books, there are also great websites like Pluralsight (*https://www.plural sight.com/*) and W3Schools (*http://www.w3schools.com/*) to gain foundational knowledge in whatever topics you choose to pursue. And never underestimate Google when you have a specific question. Chances are if you have a question or problem, someone else has probably had it too and the answer was posted online.

If you cannot find an answer to your question, there is a great Q&A site called Stack Overflow (*http://stackoverflow.com/*) filled with professionals and enthusiasts in all areas of technology. You can post a well-defined, researched question and get answers from other members for free. The most productive answerers often work for Google, Oracle, Microsoft, and other big technology companies. Some of them have written books or are Silicon Valley celebrities in the technology community. These people provide expertise simply because they are passionate about what they do.

Finally, you are more than welcome to email me if you have any questions, concerns, or comments. If you have feedback on this book or have more general questions, I can try my best to help with that. Please email me at *tmnield@outlook.com*—I look forward to hearing from you.

Happy querying!

Operators and Functions

This appendix covers common operations and functions used in SQLite as a convenient reference. While this book does not cover all the functionalities of SQLite, the functionalities likely to have an immediate need can be found here. The primary goal is to showcase universal SQL concepts that apply to most platforms, not to teach the nuances of the SQLite platform in detail.

A comprehensive coverage of SQLite's features can be found at *https://www.sqlite.org/docs.html*.

Appendix A1 – Literal Expression Queries

You can test operators and functions easily without querying any tables at all. You simply SELECT an expression of literals as in the following query, which will calculate a single value of 12:

```
SELECT 5 + 7
```

Any functions and literals, including text strings, can be tested in this manner as well. This query will check if the word 'TONY' is in the string 'TONY STARK', and it should return 1:

```
SELECT INSTR('TONY STARK', 'TONY')
```

This is a great way to test operators and functions without using any tables. This appendix will show many examples with this approach, and you can use it for your own experimentation.

Appendix A2 – Mathematical Operators

SQLite has a small set of basic math operators. More advanced tasks are usually done with functions, but here are the five core mathematical operators.

Assume x = 7 and y = 3

Operator	Description	Example	Result
+	Adds two numbers	x + y	10
-	Subtracts two numbers	x - y	4
*	Multiplies two numbers	x * y	21
/	Divides two numbers	x / y	2
%	Divides two numbers, but returns the remainder	x % y	1

Appendix A3 – Comparison Operators

Comparison operators yield a true (1) or false (0) value based on a comparative evaluation.

Assume x = 5 and y = 10

Operator	Description	Example	Result
= and ==	Checks if two values are equal	x = y	0 (false)
!= and <>	Checks if two values are not equal	x != y	1 (true)
>	Checks if value on left is greater than value on right	x > y	0 (false)
<	Checks if value on left is less than value on right	x < y	1 (true)
>=	Checks if value on left is greater than or equal to value on right	x >= y	0 (false)
<=	Checks if value on left is less than or equal to value on right	x <= y	1 (true)

APPENDIX A4 – Logical Operators

Logical operators allow you combine Boolean expressions as well as perform more conditional operations.

Assume x = true (1) and y = false (0)

Assume a = 4 and b = 10

Operator	Description	Example	Result
AND	Checks for all Boolean expressions to be true	x AND y	0 (false)
OR	Checks for any Boolean expression to be true	x OR y	1 (true)
BETWEEN	Checks if a value inclusively falls inside a range	a BETWEEN 1 and b	1 (true)

Operator	Description	Example	Result
IN	Checks if a value is in a list of values	a IN (1,5,6,7)	0 (false)
NOT	Negates and flips a Boolean expression's value	a NOT IN (1,5,6,7)	1 (true)
IS NULL	Checks if a value is null	a IS NULL	0 (false)
IS NOT NULL	Checks if a value is not null	a IS NOT NULL	1 (true)

APPENDIX A5 – Text Operators

Text has a limited set of operators, as most text processing tasks are done with functions. There are a few, though. Keep in mind also that regular expressions are beyond the scope of this book, but they are worth studying if you ever work heavily with text patterns.

Assume city = 'Dallas' and state = 'TX'

Operator	Description	Example	Result
||	Concatenates one or more values together into text	city || ', ' || state	Dallas, TX
LIKE	Allows wildcards _ and % to look for text patterns	state LIKE 'D_l%'	1 (true)
REGEXP	Matches a text pattern using a regular expression	state REGEXP '[A-Z]{2}'	1 (true)

 A special note to programmers: REGEXP is not implemented out of the box for SQLite, so you may have to compile or implement it when using SQLite for your app or program.

APPENDIX A6 – Common Core Functions

SQLite has many core functions built in. While this is not a comprehensive list, these are the most commonly used ones. A full list of functions and their documentation can be found at *http://www.sqlite.org/lang_corefunc.html*.

Assume x = –5, y = 2, and z is NULL

Operator	Description	Example	Result
abs()	Calculates the absolute value of a number	abs(x)	5
coalesce()	Converts a possible null value into a default value if it is null	coalesce(z, y)	2
instr()	Checks if a text string contains another text string; if so it returns the index for the found position, and otherwise it returns 0	instr('HTX','TX')	2
length()	Provides the number of characters in a string	length('Dallas')	6
trim()	Removes extraneous spaces on both sides of a string	trim(' TX ')	TX

Operator	Description	Example	Result
ltrim()	Removes extraneous spaces on the left side of a string	ltrim(' TX')	TX
rtrim()	Removes extraneous spaces on the right side of a string	rtrim('LA ')	LA
random()	Returns a pseudorandom number from the range −9223372036854775808 to +9223372036854775807	random()	7328249
round()	Rounds a decimal to a specified number of decimal places	round(182.245, 2)	182.24
replace()	Replaces a substring of text in a string with another string	replace('Tom Nield','Tom', 'Thomas')	Thomas Nield
substr()	Extracts a range of characters from a string with their numeric positions	substr('DOG',2,3)	OG
lower()	Turns all letters in a string to lowercase	lower('DoG')	dog
upper()	Turns all letters in a string to uppercase	upper('DoG')	DOG

APPENDIX A7 – Aggregate Functions

SQLite has a set of aggregate functions you can use with a GROUP BY statement to get a scoped aggregation in some form.

X = a column you specify the aggregation on

Function	Description
avg(X)	Calculates the average of all values in that column (omits null values).
count(X)	Counts the number of non-null values in that column.
count(*)	Counts the number of records.
max(X)	Calculates the maximum value in that column (omits null values).
min(X)	Calculates the minimum value in that column (omits null values).
sum(X)	Calculates the sum of the values in that column (omits null values).
group_concat(X)	Concatenates all non-null values in that column. You can also provide a second argument specifying a separator, like commas.

APPENDIX A8 – Date and Time Functions

Functionality for dates and times in SQL varies greatly between database platforms. Therefore, this book does not cover this topic outside this appendix. You will need to learn the date/time syntax for your specific database platform. Some platforms, such as MySQL, make working with date/time values very intuitive, while others can be less intuitive.

For SQLite, date and time functions cannot be comprehensively covered here as that would be beyond the scope of this book. But the most common date and time tasks will be covered in this section. Full documentation of SQLite date and time handling can be found at the SQLite website (*http://www.sqlite.org/lang_datefunc.html*).

Date Functions

When working with dates, it is simplest to store them in the string format YYYY-MM-DD as most database platforms inherently understand this format (technically called the ISO8601 format). A four-digit year comes first, following by a two-digit month, and a two-digit day, each separated by a dash (e.g., 2015-06-17). If you format your date strings like this, you will never have to do any explicit conversions.

When running a query, any string in the `'YYYY-MM-DD'` date format will be interpreted as a date. This means you can do chronological tasks like comparing one date to another date:

```
SELECT '2015-05-14' > '2015-01-12'
```

If you do not use this ISO8601 format, SQLite will compare them as text strings and check if the first text comes before the second text alphabetically. This obviously is not desirable as you want dates to be evaluated, compared, and treated as dates.

Conveniently, you can get today's date by passing a `'now'` string to the `DATE()` function:

```
SELECT DATE('now')
```

SQLite also allows you to pass any number of modifier arguments to the `DATE()` function. For instance, you can get yesterday's date by passing `'-1 day'` as an argument:

```
SELECT DATE('now','-1 day')
```

You can pass also pass a date string to the `DATE()` function, and add any number of modifiers to transform the date. This example will add three months and subtract one day from 2015-12-07:

```
SELECT DATE('2015-12-07','+3 month','-1 day')
```

There are several advanced date transformations you can perform. Refer to the SQLite date functions link at the beginning of this section to get a comprehensive overview of these functionalities.

Time Functions

Time also has a typical format, which is HH:MM:SS (this also is ISO8601 standard). HH is a two-digit military format of hours, MM is a two-digit format of minutes, and SS is a two-digit format of seconds . The separator is a colon. If you format times like this, the strings will always be interpreted as time values. This string represents a time value of 4:31 PM and 15 seconds:

```
SELECT '16:31:15'
```

You can omit the seconds value if you are not concerned with it. SQLite will infer the seconds value to be 00:

```
SELECT '16:31'
```

Just like with dates, you can do all kinds of operations with times, like comparing one time value to another:

```
SELECT '16:31' < '08:31'
```

The 'now' string also works with the TIME() function to get the current time:

```
SELECT TIME('now')
```

Also like with dates, you can use the TIME() function to perform transformations such as adding or subtracting hours, minutes, and seconds:

```
SELECT TIME('16:31','+1 minute')
```

Date/Time Functions

You can have a date that also has a time value. Reasonably, the standard string format is the date and time formats concatenated together, separated by a space: 'YYYY-MM-DD HH:MM:SS'. SQLite will recognize a string in this format to be a date/time value:

```
SELECT '2015-12-13 16:04:11'
```

All the rules from the DATE() and TIME() functions can apply to the DATETIME() function. You can use 'now', transformations, and any other chronological operations we have learned. For instance, you can subtract a day from a date/time value and add three hours:

```
SELECT DATETIME('2015-12-13 16:04:11','-1 day','+3 hour')
```

There are several other functions and features for working with dates and time in SQLite, including converting dates into alternative formats and compensating for times zones. There is also support for Unix time and the Julian day number system. As said earlier, go to *http://www.sqlite.org/lang_datefunc.html* to get a comprehensive list of these functionalities.

Supplementary Topics

There are some database and SQL tasks that, at the time of writing, did not fit into the mission of this book. The intention was to get your feet wet with SQL and not inundate you with every functionality available. But there are some topics that arguably do not fit into the core mission of this book, yet do not deserve to be omitted either. These are given mention here to help you progress in your proficiency.

APPENDIX B1 – Further Topics of Interest

This is a beginner's book on SQL. Therefore, the scope and focus is limited to foundational topics. However, if you finished this book and are interested in expanding your database and SQL repertoire, here are some suggested topics you can explore and research:

Topic	Description
UNION and UNION ALL	Append the results of two or more queries into a single result set.
Subqueries	Query off other queries just like they were tables.
Indexes	Improve the SELECT performance of a table with large amounts of data (addressed briefly in "APPENDIX B2 – Improving Performance with Indexes" on page 108).
Transactions	Perform multiple UPDATE/DELETE/INSERT statements as one fail-safe batch (addressed briefly in "Appendix B3 – Transactions" on page 109).
Triggers	React to UPDATE/DELETE/INSERT statements and perform tasks like logging and advanced data validation.
Regular expressions	Use a universal syntax to match advanced text patterns easily—basically, LIKE wildcards on steroids.
Database administration	Fine-tune production databases for large corporate environments.

You will probably encounter dozens of other topics, especially as you explore the nuances of different database platforms. But these should provide plenty of leads to expand your database knowledge beyond this book.

APPENDIX B2 – Improving Performance with Indexes

As your database grows, the performance can start to slow down with SELECT queries. The machine has to process each record to find ones that match your WHERE condition, and obviously having more records will slow this process down.

A common way to improve performance significantly is to use *indexes*, a mechanism that enables faster lookups in a way very similar to an index in a book. An index speeds up SELECT performance, but it slows down INSERT, UPDATE, and DELETE statements. It will also make the database file larger. These are factors you have to balance in your decision to use them. You should not think about creating indexes when you first design a database. Do it later, when you find you are having performance issues.

You specify an index on one or more columns, and you want these columns to be the ones you frequently qualify on. For example, if you frequently query the PRODUCT table and use a WHERE statement on the price column, you can apply an index on that column as shown here:

```
CREATE INDEX price_index ON PRODUCT(price);
```

We name the index price_index and we apply it on the PRODUCT table, and in parentheses we specify it on the price column. SQLite will keep a map of which records have which price values. This will significantly speed up performance when we qualify on price. But obviously, when we modify records it has to update this index, so this overhead will slow down INSERT, UPDATE, and DELETE operations.

You will notice in the SQLiteStudio database navigator that the table contains all the index objects you have created (see Figure B-1).

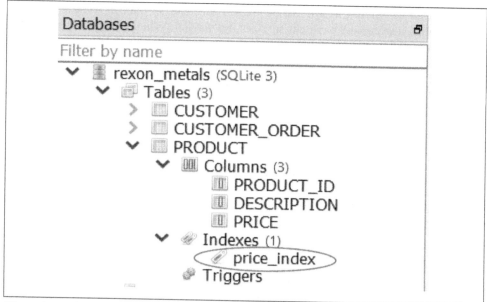

Figure B-1. The price_index was added to the PRODUCT table's indexes

You can also create a UNIQUE index for a column that never has duplicate values, and SQLite will make special optimizations for that case:

```
CREATE UNIQUE INDEX name_index ON CUSTOMER(name);
```

In addition, you can use composite indexes if two or more fields are frequently qualified together, but that is beyond the scope of this book.

To remove an index, just run a DROP INDEX statement on the index's name:

```
DROP INDEX price_index;
```

Again, indexes should only be used for very large tables that have noticeable performance issues with SELECT statements. You should avoid using indexes on small tables as the overhead will actually slow performance down (meaning this example was demonstrational, not something you should actually do to the PRODUCT table). You should also avoid using indexes on tables that update heavily and frequently.

Appendix B3 – Transactions

There may be situations where you will want to execute multiple INSERT, UPDATE, or DELETE statements as a batch, but you want all of them to complete successfully, and if one fails you want all of them to fail. This is known as *atomicity*, which means these actions must all happen successfully or none of them happen at all.

A good example where this kind of behavior is needed is financial transactions, like bank account transfers or payment services like PayPal. When you take money from one account and put it in another, you have to make sure both operations happen successfully.

Take these two INSERT statements that move $187.56 from one account and put it in another:

```
INSERT INTO ACCOUNT_ACTIVITY (ACCOUNT_ID,AMOUNT) VALUES (1563,-187.56);

INSERT INTO ACCOUNT_ACTIVITY (ACCOUNT_ID,AMOUNT) VALUES (3067,187.56);
```

What happens if the first INSERT succeeds but the second one fails? Well, that $187.56 has effectively disappeared. You have two upset customers and a possible auditing mess. So how do you ensure that in the event of failure, that money returns back to the customer giving it and everything is restored to the way it was?

The answer is to leverage a *transaction*. With a transaction you can make this transfer atomic and do a ROLLBACK if anything fails and a COMMIT if everything succeeds.

First, call the BEGIN or BEGIN TRANSACTION command (these are the same command):

```
BEGIN TRANSACTION;
```

Now any INSERT, UPDATE, and DELETE statements will be recorded so they can be undone if necessary. Perform the two INSERTs. The actions will be performed while being recorded in "transaction mode":

```
INSERT INTO ACCOUNT_ACTIVITY (ACCOUNT_ID,AMOUNT) VALUES (1563,-187.56);

INSERT INTO ACCOUNT_ACTIVITY (ACCOUNT_ID,AMOUNT) VALUES (3067,187.56);
```

If everything goes well and no errors occurred, you can call COMMIT or its alias, END TRANSACTION, to finalize the INSERTs. The transfer has then happened successfully.

Now let's start another transaction so we can do another transfer:

```
BEGIN TRANSACTION;
```

However, this time we are going to break it. Say we do another transfer between these two accounts:

```
INSERT INTO ACCOUNT_ACTIVITY (ACCOUNT_ID,AMOUNT) VALUES (1563,-121.36);

INSERT INTO ACCOUNT_ACTIVITY (ACCOUNT_ID,AMOUNT) VALUES (121.36);
```

The first statement will succeed, but the second SQL statement was messed up and will error out. It is missing the ACCOUNT_ID value, and now we have $121.36 in limbo.

Fortunately, we are in "transaction mode." We can basically hit a rewind button and call ROLLBACK. This will undo everything since the last COMMIT or BEGIN TRANSACTION we called. The first INSERT will be undone and the $121.36 will be back in the 1563 account.

In the event that a database connection goes down, a bad SQL statement is composed, or a validation rule train-wrecks a series of updates, transactions are a way to ensure data does not get corrupted in your database. You will especially want to use them with automated processes or large jobs requiring you INSERT, UPDATE, and DELETE a high volume of fragile records.

Index

literal expression queries, 101
logical operators, 102

M

mathematical operators, 26, 102
MAX() function, 44, 50
Microsoft Access, 5
MIN() function, 50
modulus operator (%), 32
MySQL, 7

N

names in SQL
    underscore(_) in, 25
    using aliases, 24
non-null values, counting in a column, 42
normalization, 4
NOT IN statement, 32
Not NULL constraint, 79
null values
    aggregate functions and, 43
    and Boolean values in tables, 83
    converting to zeros with coalesce(), 65
    in LEFT JOINs versus INNER JOINs, 65
    resulting from LEFT JOIN, checking for, 60
    zero/null CASE trick, 49-52

O

one-to-many relationships, 54
operators
    comparison, 102
    concatenation, 27
    logical, 102
    mathematical, 26, 102
    text, 103
OR statement, 32
ORDER BY operator, 41
order of operations, 37
ordinal positions, 41, 49
OUTER JOIN operator, 61

P

parent-child relationships, 54
performance, improving with indexes, 108
PRIMARY KEY constraint, 81, 92
primary keys, 70
    defining in SQLiteStudio, 78
    in SQLite, 82

programming languages, resources for, 98
Python, learning more about, 98

Q

Query Results pane (SQLiteEditor), 19

R

R language, learning more about, 98
relational database management system
    (RDBMS), 3
relational databases, 3
relationships between tables, 54
    and joining multiple tables, 61
    in the database schema, 71
RIGHT JOIN operator, 61
ROLLBACK command, 110
rolling up data, 39
round() function, 26, 43

S

schemas (database), 71
security questions (database design), 68
SELECT statement, 19-28
    DISTINCT operator, 46
    executing before DELETEs, 94
    expressions in, 23
    inserting records using results from, 93
    literal expression queries, 101
    specifying columns for, 21
    spreading across multiple lines, 24
    storing frequently used SELECT queries in a
        database, 86
    text concatenation in, 27
    writing and executing in SQLiteStudio, 20
semicolon (;), ending SQL statements, 22
servers, 6
SET keyword, 95
software development, 98
spaces in SQL names, underscore(_) as place-
    holder, 25
SQL
    database solutions, 5
    marketability of, 1
    resources for further learning, 97
    uses of, 2
SQL injection, 68
SQL Work Area (SQLiteStudio), 10
SQLite, 5, 9-17

About the Author

Thomas Nield has a business analyst background and works in revenue management at Southwest Airlines. Early in his career, he became fascinated with technology and bought dozens of books to master programming in Java, C#, and database design. He is passionate about sharing what he learns and enabling others with new skillsets, even if they do not work in IT. He enjoys making technical content relatable and relevant to those unfamiliar with or intimidated by it.

Colophon

The animal on the cover of *Getting Started with SQL* is a Natterjack toad (*Epidalea calamita*). It is part of the Bufonidae family and can be found in sand dune systems, heathlands, and coastlines with low coverings of grass throughout western European.

An identifying feature of natterjack toads is the yellow line that runs down the middle of their backs. Adults range in length from 50–70 mm, with females being larger than males. Overall coloring is either brown, cream, or green, and they are covered in warts, like their toad brethren. Another distinguishing feature is its shorter hind legs, which make it more of a runner than a hopper or walker, as other toads are.

Like more common toads, the natterjack diet consists of many invertebrate insects such as beetles, spiders, and worms. They are nocturnal hunters, so meals are swallowed whole at night. Those in sand dune systems are also known to eat small crustaceans, such as freshwater shrimp. Natterjacks release toxins from their skin, which make them unlikely to be made into meals themselves, but birds such as grey herons, as well as grass snakes are able to consume them without issue.

As with hunting, the natterjack's mating rituals are nocturnal. Males have a dinstinct, loud mating call that signals females to head to nearby warm, shallow waters (because natterjacks are terrible swimmers). This usually occurs between the months of April and July, with females spawning 1,500–7,500 eggs. The eggs turn into tadpoles about a week after fertilization, which then turn into toadlets 3–8 weeks later.

Many of the animals on O'Reilly covers are endangered; all of them are important to the world. To learn more about how you can help, go to *animals.oreilly.com*.

The cover image is from *Johnson's Natural History*. The cover fonts are URW Typewriter and Guardian Sans. The text font is Adobe Minion Pro; the heading font is Adobe Myriad Condensed; and the code font is Dalton Maag's Ubuntu Mono.

Get even more for your money.

Join the O'Reilly Community, and register the O'Reilly books you own. It's free, and you'll get:

- $4.99 ebook upgrade offer
- 40% upgrade offer on O'Reilly print books
- Membership discounts on books and events
- Free lifetime updates to ebooks and videos
- Multiple ebook formats, DRM FREE
- Participation in the O'Reilly community
- Newsletters
- Account management
- 100% Satisfaction Guarantee

Signing up is easy:

1. Go to: oreilly.com/go/register
2. Create an O'Reilly login.
3. Provide your address.
4. Register your books.

Note: English-language books only

To order books online:
oreilly.com/store

For questions about products or an order:
orders@oreilly.com

To sign up to get topic-specific email announcements and/or news about upcoming books, conferences, special offers, and new technologies:
elists@oreilly.com

For technical questions about book content:
booktech@oreilly.com

To submit new book proposals to our editors:
proposals@oreilly.com

O'Reilly books are available in multiple DRM-free ebook formats. For more information:
oreilly.com/ebooks

Have it your way.

6-16

CPSIA information can be obtained at www.ICGtesting.com
Printed in the USA
BVOW07s0244120216

436350BV00001B/2/P

9 781491 938614